The Human Aspects of Project Management

Organizing Projects for Success

The Human Aspects of Project Management

Volume One:
Organizing Projects for Success

Volume Two:
Human Resource Skills for Project Managers

Volume Three:
Managing the Project Team

The Human Aspects of Project Management

Organizing Projects for Success

Vijay K. Verma, P. Eng., M.B.A.

Project Management Institute
130 South State Road
Upper Darby, PA 19082
610/734-3330

Library of Congress Cataloging-in-Publication Data

Verma, Vijay K., (1949–   )
    The human aspects of project management / Vijay K. Verma.
        p.   cm.
    Includes bibliographical references and index
    Contents: v. 1. Organizing projects for success
    ISBN: 1-880410-40-0 (pbk. : alk. paper)
    1. Industrial project management. 2. Matrix organization.
3. Work groups. I. Title.
HD69.P75V47 1995
658.4'04--dc20   95-40579
                                                                 CIP

Editor-in-Chief: James S. Pennypacker
Copyeditor: Jeannette Cabanis
Cover design by: Dewey L. Messer
Book design by: Michelle Triggs

PMI books are available at special quantity discounts to use as
premiums and sales promotions, or for use in corporate
training programs. For more information, please write to the
Business Manager, PMI Communications, Colonial Square,
323 West Main Street, Sylva, NC 28779. Or contact your
local bookstore.

The paper used in this book complies with the Permanent
Paper Standard issued by the National Information Standards
Organization (Z39.48—1984).

10   9   8   7   6   5   4   3   2   1

Table of Contents

5

Foreword to the *Human Aspects of Project Management* Series

Today's ever-changing business environment requires new approaches to project management, which has become an important tool for dealing with time-to-market, resource limitations, downsizing, and global competition. As markets and project organizations become more dynamic, administrative and technical skills alone are no longer sufficient to deal with the complexities of modern project undertakings. Project managers who want to compete on a world-class level must understand the human side of their organizations and business processes. They must be social architects who can work across levels and functions of the organization, continuously improving the business process and fostering an ambiance conducive to innovation, risk-taking, self-directed teamwork, commitment, quality and self-improvement.

The *Human Aspects of Project Management* series offers project managers and their teams the conceptual and practical guidelines for leading people effectively and confidently towards challenging project objectives. The series goes beyond the traditional, linear approach to project management, which assumes that project budgets and schedules can always be clearly defined and can form the cornerstone for tracking and controlling a project. By focusing on the human side, Verma offers a fresh approach to modern project management. He shows how to unleash higher levels of creativity, productivity, quality and commitment from the project team by considering the human aspects.

With these books, the seasoned management practitioner or scholar who understands the conventional tools and techniques of project management but wants to go beyond the basic framework can gain a better understanding of the factors that drive project performance. *The Human Aspects of Project Management* provides a conceptual construct for managing modern projects. It offers concrete suggestions for dealing with diverse project teams, issues of delegation, empowerment, accountability, control, commitment, organizational linkages, alliances, and the intricacies of matrix management. Perhaps most important, the concepts set forth in this series will allow project leaders to build a true project team, which includes alliances with the business organization, support groups, and project sponsors. Such a project team establishes the foundation for an effective and productive project management system that can solve complex problems and produce quality results.

— Hans J. Thamhain, Ph.D.
Bentley College

Preface

Always remember that your own resolution to succeed is more important than anything else.

— Abraham Lincoln

Tough global competition, rapidly changing technology and dynamic market situations have forced business and industrial organizations to exploit new opportunities and management approaches. All these dramatic changes have accelerated the growth and acceptance of project management concepts and philosophies. Projects are the building blocks for developing industrial, commercial, and infrastructure facilities and organizations. "Management by project" is now regarded as a competitive way of managing organizations. Such management involves organizing the majority of organizational objectives and initiatives as projects, then managing them using effective project management strategies and techniques.

In general, project management refers to the management of discrete projects, with identifiable objectives, limited resources, and a finite time duration. To plan and monitor projects under these constraints, project management emphasizes the effective integration of people, technology, and tasks, along with a practical and efficient management system. Extensive literature dealing with the conventional tools and techniques of corporate human resource management is readily available. What is not so readily available is literature addressing the range of human resource issues as they relate to the project environment. This book attempts to fill that need.

Why This Series of Books?

Managing projects requires unique skills and techniques, different from those needed to manage ongoing operations. As project management moves into the 21st century, project managers face the challenges of operating in a project environment characterized by high levels of uncertainty, cross-cultural teams, and global competition for competent human resources. These challenges can be met by developing a clear understanding of human factors in project management and by effective use of the human resource management skills that are required to inspire project stakeholders to work together in order to meet project objectives.

Extensive literature and many software packages are available for the traditional aspects of project management: planning, scheduling, and reporting; cost control and risk analysis; and management of scope and quality. Yet most project managers agree that the real management challenges lie not in technical problems but in the behavioral and organizational aspects of projects.

We sometimes forget that, despite the recent information and technology revolution in project management, people are at the center of projects. People determine the success or failure of a project. They define project goals. They plan, organize, direct, coordinate, and monitor project activities. They meet project goals and objectives by using interpersonal and organizational skills such as communication, delegation, decision making and negotiation. In project environments, people can be viewed as problems and constraints—or as solutions and opportunities.

Human resource management is therefore a vital component of project management. Many books on general management, personnel management, and organizational behavior contain concepts and techniques that support project management. But understanding the myriad complex human factors that determine project success requires research and experience specific to the project environment. The Project Management Institute has played a leadership role in this area by developing practical and thought-provoking literature and the *Project Management Body of Knowledge,* which includes human resource management as one of the eight knowledge areas. This series gathers together these and many other resources on the human aspects of management. It focuses on making the most of human resources on projects. The emphasis is on people and how they can be organized to increase their overall effectiveness as individuals, as project teams, and as members of organizations.

Throughout my working life, I have always been fascinated by the degree to which human factors influence the success of project management. The ideas presented in this series developed from years of study and research; from my practical experience at TRIUMF; and from discussions with friends, colleagues, other project management professionals, consultancy clients, and those who have attended my classes and seminars.

9

These ideas are not likely to become the last word in human factors in project management, but I hope they will incite an increased awareness, just as the efforts of researchers and project management practitioners who have successfully implemented creative leadership motivated me to think further about effective project human resources management. Project management will be more successful, and my efforts in writing this series well rewarded, if project management educators and practitioners are inspired to devote more energy to this important area.

One final note: As you read, you may occasionally come across a concept or an idea that you feel you already know. That may be true indeed. As Somerset Maugham said, "Basic truths are too important to be new."

About This Book

Volume 1: Organizing Projects for Success

People who get ahead are those who prove they can get things done.
— *David Kearns*

How *do* project managers "get things done"? Project managers typically have substantial responsibility and accountability but very limited authority. Therefore, they are dependent upon cooperation from all project stakeholders: the client, project team members, functional managers, support personnel, and other external stakeholders. They must be able to organize their projects by using organizational and human skills to achieve effective integration of all resources and functions.

Understanding issues of authority, accountability, reliability and responsibility; gaining the commitment of project participants; knowing how to delegate effectively—all these are critical to good project management, and are discussed at length in this volume. Yet even the best human skills can be hampered by an organizational structure that does not support management by projects. Therefore, the crucial step of organizing a project is emphasized, with a special focus on matrix organizational structure.

Through this book, I would like to share with readers my ideas about managing projects in a way characterized by dignity, purpose, vision, and competitive advantage. I hope you will enjoy reading this book and use it for years to come as a reference for managing projects *successfully* by managing project human resources *effectively*.

Who should read this book? "Management by projects" is now regarded as a competitive way to manage all types of organizations. By addressing the human aspects of project management and important issues of human resource management in a project mode, the book should help anyone—from project management academics and practitioners to a novice in the field. It will help project management professionals who are interested in learning the human skills to interface with major stakeholders, in developing appropriate organizational design strategies, or in the effective team building that achieves human synergy. It will help top management, project managers, team members, internal and external stakeholders, and other project participants (functional managers, support personnel, etc.) increase their effectiveness in organizing projects and in meeting project objectives. Project management educators can use this book to develop a short course, seminar, or training workshop.

The ideas presented here apply to projects in any industry, including conventional construction, utilities, transportation, defense, manufacturing, petrochemical, service industries, information systems and technology, computer and communications, pharmaceutical, education, research and development, high-tech, financial, hospitality, films, and the arts.

The topics in this book are organized in such a way that readers can easily find their particular areas of interest. No previous knowledge in organizational behavior is required, but a keen interest in project management will be useful to understand thoroughly and apply the concepts presented. Each chapter deals with important aspects of project human resource management and outlines practical guidelines for managing those areas successfully. The concepts and ideas are illustrated by figures and the main points highlighted by bullets.

Learning objectives. After reading this book and relevant reference material, readers will have an understanding of:

- What project human resource management is and how it relates to the project life cycle
- A model for effective management of project human resources emphasizing three key factors: communication, teamwork, and leadership
- The effect of cultural ambiance on project management
- Interfacing with the client/owner, contractors and subcontractors
- Identifying, classifying and interfacing with internal and external project stakeholders
- Issues of authority, responsibility, reliability, and accountability in a project environment and balancing these to gain everyone's commitment
- Effective delegation (obstacles and guidelines)
- Project management factors and forces influencing project organizations
- Organization/authority continuum and project structures
- Various types of project structures (functional, weak to strong matrix, fully projectized, and task force)
- Matrix structures (types, why and when to use matrix)
- Pros and cons of matrix, and making matrix work

Minds are like parachutes; they function best when open!

— *Anonymous*

12

Acknowledgments

Writing this book has been a labor of love. Like many challenges in life, writing requires diligence, perseverance, patience, and discipline—characteristics that don't come easily to many of us, and I am no exception. However, I am very fortunate to have people who encouraged me to stay on track and finish this book, despite many rewrites.

This book would not have been possible without the help of my friend, colleague, and mentor, R. Max Wideman, who stood by me throughout this project. If I acknowledge all Max's ideas and discussions, his name will be all over this book. Max helped me a great deal in developing my views, reviewing my manuscript, and discussing the topics covered. I cannot repay Max for the extraordinary amount of time he devoted to this project.

Another whose help was invaluable is Raso Samarasekera, who entered my handwritten manuscript into the computer. She went through several revisions cheerfully, with special attention to detail and quality. In addition, my colleague Mark Keyzer helped tremendously by discussing ideas and preparing all figures and tables.

I am also grateful to Dr. Francis M. Webster, Jr., who encouraged me to stay with this project and played a significant role in expediting it. He reviewed my manuscript and gave me many thought-provoking comments. I wish also to thank Jim Pennypacker, Editor-in-Chief, PMI Communications; Jeannette Cabanis, who edited my manuscript; and Michelle Triggs, the book designer. The PMI Communications staff helped me to close this project in a very professional manner.

I also wish to thank Dr. Dundar Kocaoglu, Dr. Jaclyn Kostner, members of the PMI West Coast B.C. Chapter, and my colleagues at TRIUMF with whom I shared my ideas and who gave me moral support in this endeavor. I especially wish to acknowledge the senior management members of TRIUMF—Dr. Erich Vogt, Dr. Alan Astbury, and Dr. Ewart Blackmore for their continuous support. Thanks are also owed to the participants in my classes and seminars for their excellent ideas and discussions.

On a personal level, I would like to thank my late parents and Taya Ji; my brothers, Rajinder and Sudesh Verma and their spouses; my sisters, Prem and Sangeeta and their spouses; my in-laws; and my special friends, Raksha and K.L. Toky. Although they are thousands of miles away, they have always inspired me in this endeavor.

Finally, special thanks to my daughters Serena and Angelee and my son Naveen, who supported me, suggested ideas about the basics of understanding people, and gave me an opportunity to complete this book while wondering what Daddy was doing at night in his study room. Most of all, I am indebted to my wife, Shiksha Verma, for her love, understanding, and support. All that I am today, I owe to her love, friendship, and devotion. She does not truly know the extent to which she has helped me in completing this project. Shiksha, my appreciation for your support and love cannot be expressed in words, but thanks many times.

Vijay K. Verma
June 1995

Outline

The secret of success in life is for a man to be ready for his time when it comes.

— Benjamin Disraeli

Human Resource Management and Project Management

INDUSTRIAL AND BUSINESS organizations are fighting for survival in a world characterized by technological advancements, dynamic markets, tough global competition, and complex organizational structures. Because organizational success depends in large part on the successful completion of projects, organizations today are placing a higher priority than ever before on implementing project management strategies and techniques.

Most project management professionals agree that one of the toughest challenges they face is managing human resources effectively. Projects in all sectors and industries involve people with a diverse mix of backgrounds, skills, and expectations. People determine the success and failure of a project. People, if they are committed and enthusiastic about the project, the way it is organized, and the project's human resource management climate, will turn *ordinary* performance into *extraordinary* performance.

Human resource management is a vital component of project management. Although concepts and techniques used in project human resource management and general management are very similar in broad terms, they have to be implemented somewhat differently. In a project environment, project managers are expected to meet specific project objectives within specified scope, quality, time, and cost constraints. Successful management of projects requires a balanced mix of technical, human, and conceptual skills. ■

About Projects and Project Management

There are no secrets to success. It is the result of preparation, hard work and learning from failure.

— *Gen. Colin Powell in* The Black Collegian

Projects play a vital role in the development of many organizations. They come in many different sizes and are found in both business and industrial environments, including conventional construction and engineering; defense and aerospace; public sector (utilities, government, and transportation); research and development; high-tech, computer, and communications; pulp and paper; petrochemical; general manufacturing; and other specialized areas such as finance, tourism, the arts, etc. The survival and growth of most of these organizations depends upon their ability to manage their projects.

The Project Management Institute has developed a *Project Management Body of Knowledge (PMBOK)* that describes a collection of knowledge within the profession of project management. The *PMBOK* includes proven, traditional practices that are widely applied, as well as innovative and advanced ones that have seen more limited use. It encompasses topics, subject areas, and intellectual processes involved in the application of sound management principles to the collective execution of efforts that qualify as projects. These principles overlap with general management principles for functions such as planning, organizing, executing, and monitoring.

Projects and the project life cycle

Projects have been in existence for a long time. Various definitions of a "project" have been attempted. For example:

- A project is any undertaking that has definite, final objectives that represent specified values to satisfy some need or desire. It is normally characterized by limitations placed on time, cost, and resources such as people, skills, equipment, and materials.
- A project is a cluster of activities that is relatively separate and clear-cut. It has a distinct mission and a clear termination point. A project might be a part of a broader program, yet its main theme lies in identifying a nice, neat work package within a bewildering array of objectives, alternatives, and activities.

The Project Management Body of Knowledge defines a project as:[1]

- A temporary endeavor undertaken to create a unique product or service. *Temporary* means that every project has a definite ending point and *unique* means that the product or service differs in some distinguishing way from all similar products or services.

These definitions concur that projects are typically unique and are characterized by a well-defined set of objectives to be met within limited resources and time constraints. A project may involve a single person or

16

department, or it may involve several people cutting across several functional or organizational boundaries, as in joint ventures and partnerships. A project can be viewed as a vehicle through which change can be created and successfully managed, using appropriate human skills and the project management practices outlined in the *PMBOK*. However, it may present a challenge to the status quo and be seen as a threat. Typical examples of projects include:[1]

- Developing a new product or service
- Implementing a change in structure, staffing, and style of an organization
- Designing new transportation, vehicle, and/or defense systems
- Constructing a building facility, highway, plant, railways, etc.
- Developing a new or modified information and communication system
- Developing and marketing a new drug
- Manufacturing a new piece of machinery, equipment, etc.
- Running a campaign for political office and/or raising funds
- Implementing a new business procedure or process.

Most projects require a combination of organizational resources, assembled together to create something unique that will contribute to the development and execution of organizational strategy.

Project life cycle. Projects have a distinct life cycle, starting with an idea and progressing through planning and development of the concept, execution, and eventual transfer to the client/customer or project owner. This sequence is collectively known as the *project life cycle*. Project life cycle is defined by the *PMBOK* as the sequential phases through which any project progresses. A project phase is marked by completion of one or more deliverables. The number and names of these phases are determined by the control needs of the organization and may be further broken down into stages, depending on the area of project application. A generic project life cycle consists of four phases: concept; development (detail planning); execution (implementation or operation); and finishing (termination or closeout).[1]

These phases may be called by different names in different environments and may even overlap, depending upon the nature and size of the project and its industrial or business environment.

What is project management?

According to PMI, project management involves applying knowledge, skills, tools, and techniques to project activities in order to meet or exceed stakeholder needs and expectations. It is the art of directing and coordinating human and material resources throughout the life of a project to achieve project objectives within specified constraints.[1]

Since projects are done by people, the five "people" areas that require special project management skills and represent necessary pre-conditions for project success are:

- Managing through effective communication in a multi-disciplinary project environment
- Building effective teams at various organizational levels to suit the project life cycle
- Managing change through effective leadership and analytical skills
- Understanding the importance of cultural ambiance in managing conflicts and other project problems effectively
- Dealing with problems across functional lines using effective interpersonal skills.

All projects are characterized by objectives, constraints, interfaces, and interactions. The *PMBOK* defines modern project management as the current broad range of project management encompassing eight major knowledge areas that focus on project management and integration. These eight areas (management of scope, quality, time, cost, risk, human resources, contract procurement, and communications) make *modern* project management distinguishable from *traditional* project management, which focuses mainly on cost, time, and product performance.[1] The following basic overview describes project interfaces and the eight knowledge areas of project management.

Project interfaces. Managing project interfaces is a major component of project management. An effectively interfaced project is a well-managed project. Interface management differs from project management in the sense that interface management is only a subset of overall project management. It addresses only the boundary issues or potential grey areas of responsibilities, which, if not interfaced adequately, can lead to problems and frustrations.

There are three main types of project interfaces:

People interfaces relate to human behavior. Managing personal interfaces requires respecting boundaries between people, overcoming behavioral barriers, and closing the gaps between people who must interact to do their work.

Organizational interfaces relate to the flow of information and communication between different components of the project organization.

Systems interfaces are non-people interfaces such as project hardware, software, facility, etc. They include the physical interconnections of subsystems and their performance criteria to integrate with the overall system.

Human skills are essential for managing all people interfaces. Project managers must recognize and continually monitor and manage these interfaces. Similarly, organizational interfacing is accomplished through people. Even system interfaces, which may appear to be "non-people" in nature, can be managed effectively by people-oriented management. The challenges faced by the project manager in interfacing with the project stakeholders, which can also be met by using effective human skills, will be discussed later.

Eight knowledge areas of project management. Project management is a dynamic process. According to PMI, it encompasses eight major knowledge areas that must be thoroughly understood in order to manage projects successfully. The project management process emphasizes the management of four core elements: scope, quality, time, and cost. These elements represent the client/customer's project objectives and emphasize *what* is to be achieved and what are the *constraints* from the perspective of the project manager.

In addition, there are four interface elements (also known as the four interactive or facilitative management functions): management of communications/information, contract/procurement, human resources, and risk. Facilitative functions provide the *means* for accomplishing project objectives and emphasize *how* objectives will be achieved.

In a typical project environment, project managers must analyze and manage all eight knowledge areas of the project management process. This typically involves trade-offs within the first set of four areas/elements plus effective management and integration of the second set of four facilitative functions.

Managing trade-offs between scope, quality, time, and cost is the key to successful project management. It means *getting the job done* and achieving a satisfactory outcome on time and at reasonable cost. Scope must encompass functional specifications, design specifications, and global constraints. Effective scope management sets the stage for project management success, yet the four goals of scope, quality, time, and cost are generally in direct conflict with each other throughout the life of the project. For example, when faced with projected cost overruns and schedule delays, a contractor may try to compromise on scope and/or quality. In R&D the scientists involved in the design and construction of research facilities are also the clients (that is, the end users) of project results and are therefore unwilling to compromise on scope or quality. In such cases, scope and quality are not compromised even if there are cost overruns and delays, provided that these can be reasonably justified. Therefore, the project manager has to recognize and balance all four factors.

Managing facilitative functions involves managing communication/information, contract/procurement, human resources, and risk. These four facilitative/integrative functions are also interrelated. In real life, project scope is rarely defined clearly at the beginning of the project and this automatically increases the potential for conflicts and project risks. However, project managers can still manage the project reasonably effectively through analysis, evaluation and application of the four facilitative functions, but above all by using effective human resource management skills and communication.[6]

In order to manage a project successfully, it is important to understand project management process and strategies in terms of:

- Purpose and objectives (review and analysis)
- Identification and analysis of strengths, weaknesses, opportunities and threats
- Issues analysis (policies, external environment, etc.)
- Stakeholder analysis (identification and management)
- Cost/benefit analysis and risk analysis (identification and management)
- Organizational design strategies (options and adaptability)
- Impact on total quality or performance (definition and measurement)
- Project human resource management strategies (interpersonal skills and relationships).

The project management process must integrate both sets of functions throughout the project life cycle with the aim of satisfying all project stakeholders according to pre-defined project requirements.

Using Human Resource Management to Manage Projects

Through human resource planning, management prepares to have the right people at the right places at the right times to fulfill both organizational and individual objectives.

— *James W. Walker*

In the past, most projects have been managed as technical systems instead of behavioral systems. Consequently, the technical aspects of project management have been highly developed, while the equal or greater gains likely to be achieved from effective management of human resources have not been realized. All projects are accomplished by people, regardless of the type of industry or the project. The majority of project management problems—schedule delays, differing priorities, poor client interface, poor communication—are behavioral rather than technical in nature. Most project managers recognize that a clear understanding of human behavior and the organizational dimensions of project management are the keys to managing projects effectively.

What is project human resource management?

The *PMBOK* defines project human resource management as the processes required to make the most effective use of the people involved with the project. It includes all the project stakeholders: clients, owners, sponsors, individual contributors, and others.[1]

Human resource managers direct and coordinate human resources by applying behavioral and administrative knowledge to achieve predetermined objectives of scope, cost, time, quality, and participant satisfaction. They deal mainly with organizational planning, staff acquisition, and team development.[1] Participants must include project stakeholders, because projects succeed only when the stakeholders are satisfied with the results or outcome.

There is a substantial body of general management literature on dealing with people in an ongoing, operational context. This literature includes many topics of common interest to the fields of general management and project management: leadership, communication, power/influence, motivation, negotiation, conflict and stress management, delegating, team building, change management and the administrative areas of human resource management (recruitment, labor relations, performance appraisals, and so on). Although a knowledge of these topics is broadly applicable to managing project human resources effectively, project managers and project team members must also be sensitive to how this knowledge and related skills specifically apply in a project environment.

Project managers and project management teams seldom have direct responsibility and control over the administrative aspects of project human resource management. Generally, in multi-project environments and for big projects requiring a large number of personnel for a longer time, personnel or human resource departments are responsible for these administrative aspects. Although this series focuses primarily on behavioral rather than administrative aspects of human resource management, project personnel should be aware of the following aspects so they can comply with required corporate policies, procedures, and regulations.

- Employee relations, recruitment, selection and job placement; personnel training, records management, and labor relations
- Compensation (salary and benefits administration)
- Performance appraisals and evaluations
- Government regulations (discrimination and equal opportunity law), union contract negotiations and arbitration.

Project success or failure depends upon human resources. Therefore, it is essential to understand the human aspects of project management. Two premises provide cornerstones of these human aspects.[8]

1. People influence a project's success or failure; and
2. A project's problems can only be solved by people.

Wilemon and Baker reviewed the following areas of key research and contribution to the understanding of the human aspects and interpersonal dimensions of project management:

- Team-building skills and decision-making styles
- Project team relationships with the parent, client, and other external organizations
- Organizational design and the project manager's authority relationship with the project participants and stakeholders
- Communications and perceptions in project management
- Leadership styles and interpersonal skills
- Conflict management.

Additional human dimensions of effective project management include motivation, trust, stress management, power/influence and politics, managing change, and cultural diversity.

Human resource management and the project life cycle

Just as costs and cash flow fluctuate significantly through the project life cycle, both in total and in terms of the allocation to various work packages, so the need for human resources and various kinds of expertise and specialization also fluctuates. The types of personnel and expertise for various phases of the project (from conception to termination) depend upon the varying nature of tasks, maturity level of project team members, and external and internal constraints. For purposes of illustration, a typical project life cycle consists of four generic phases: concept, development, execution, and finish, as shown in Figure 1.1. This figure also shows major activities, the corresponding type of personnel, and organizational design strategies for different phases of the project. The project manager must ensure that the appropriate level of skill and experience is available during each of the phases of the project life cycle. If necessary, outside help must be sought if neither the project manager nor the project team possess a required type or level of expertise.

The Project Manager and Important Project Management Skills

If one advances confidently in the direction of his dreams, and endeavors to live the life one has imagined, one will meet with a success unexpected.
— Henry David Thoreau

Project managers may have different formal titles depending upon the industry, type, size, and complexity of the project. Examples include project leader, project/program manager, project/program coordinator, task force chairman, construction manager, and so on. These titles differ mainly in terms of the relative level of formal organizational authority assigned to them. However, each of them has a fundamental responsibility to foster project integration. The attributes, skills, and responsibilities of the project manager, as often spelled out in the job description, are monumental.

This section presents an overview of a typical project manager along with his or her traits, objectives, typical responsibilities and major roles. Some practical project management skills including basic management skills, interpersonal skills, and challenges in integrating and interfacing with major stakeholders, are outlined. Also, a model for effective management of project human resources, emphasizing teamwork, leadership, communication, and cultural ambiance is presented.

About project managers

Give me a stock clerk with a goal and I will give you a person who will make history. Give me a person without a goal and I will give you a stock clerk.
— J.C. Penney

Project managers must be high achievers because they are required to complete their projects within time, cost, and performance constraints. According to Kerzner,[11] their primary responsibility is to coordinate and integrate project activities across multiple functional lines. Therefore,

Organizing Projects for Success

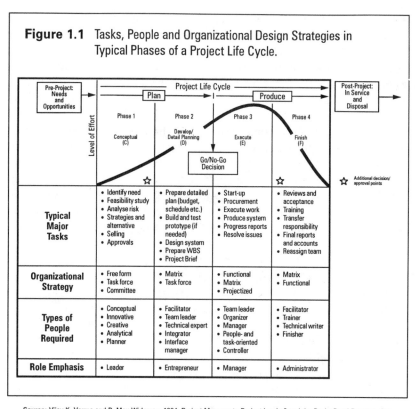

Figure 1.1 Tasks, People and Organizational Design Strategies in Typical Phases of a Project Life Cycle.

	Phase 1 Conceptual (C)	Phase 2 Develop/ Detail Planning (D)	Phase 3 Execute (E)	Phase 4 Finish (F)
Typical Major Tasks	• Identify need • Feasibility study • Analyse risk • Strategies and alternative • Selling • Approvals	• Prepare detailed plan (budget, schedule etc.) • Build and test prototype (if needed) • Design system • Prepare WBS • Project Brief	• Start-up • Procurement • Execute work • Produce system • Progress reports • Resolve issues	• Reviews and acceptance • Training • Transfer responsibility • Final reports and accounts • Reassign team
Organizational Strategy	• Free form • Task force • Committee	• Matrix • Task force	• Functional • Matrix • Projectized	• Matrix • Functional
Types of People Required	• Conceptual • Innovative • Creative • Analytical • Planner	• Facilitator • Team leader • Technical expert • Integrator • Interface manager	• Team leader • Organizer • Manager • People- and task-oriented • Controller	• Facilitator • Trainer • Technical writer • Finisher
Role Emphasis	• Leader	• Entrepreneur	• Manager	• Administrator

Source: Vijay K. Verma and R. Max Wideman. 1994. Project Manager to Project Leader? and the Rocky Road Between. *Proceedings of the 25th Annual Seminar/Symposium of the Project Management Institute.* Upper Darby, PA: Project Management Institute, pp. 627-633.

project managers should also have a general knowledge of the technology involved and its boundaries and limitations. In managing highly uncertain and "high-tech" projects, such as in research and development or in pharmaceutical industries, a command of the technology may be required, rather than just a general understanding. To meet project goals, project managers must become familiar with the operations and strengths of all functional departments and must have strong communicating, integrating, interfacing, basic management, and interpersonal skills.

Traits of project managers. Project managers are generally ambitious and self-motivated. To succeed, they must be very effective in interpersonal relations, building and nurturing project teams, administration, and problem solving. The successful project manager exhibits:
- The ability to direct and recognize good performance
- The knowledge of sufficient disciplines to be managed
- A balanced multi-disciplinary orientation
- Analytical, integrating, problem solving, and decision-making skills

- People skills: communication, motivation, and negotiation
- Energy, enthusiasm, and even temperament
- Self-confidence, reliability, maturity, and emotional stability
- A constructive, positive attitude
- Independence tempered by political awareness
- Flexibility and tolerance for ambiguity and uncertainty
- A sense of humor.

In a nutshell, project managers must have a balanced mix of determination to succeed, appreciation for project team members, and a sense of vision.

Objectives of project managers. The primary objective of project managers is to meet the project objectives. They should also aim to achieve professional growth and skills, establish good working relationships and networks, assist in the development of project team members, and above all enjoy their work. In this context, typical objectives of a project manager can be summarized as follows:

- To attain the willing commitment of people to assigned tasks
- To achieve the coordination and collaboration of different work groups, responsibility centers, and entire organizations, including that of the owner
- To achieve visibility by placing a high premium on reliability and timeliness of information, and a high cost on unnecessary or irrelevant information
- To steer the project to completion in an orderly and progressive manner
- To ensure that trade-offs between scope, cost, and time are satisfactory and acceptable, and are seen to be so
- To perpetuate development of personal and professional skills and the potential of project team members.

Typical roles of project managers. Project managers are expected to get things done as effectively and efficiently as possible. To achieve project objectives, they must use their professional skills and abilities and play many roles in integrating the efforts of their project teams. The major roles of a project manager can be classified as:

- Interpersonal roles as a figurehead, a leader, and a liaison
- Informational roles for assembling, selecting, monitoring and disseminating information, and acting as a project spokesperson
- Decisional roles for allocating resources, exploring new opportunities, handling disturbances and conflicts, negotiating, analyzing situations, setting priorities, and making sound and timely decisions to encourage creativity and progress.

Responsibilities of project managers. John Steinbeck once wrote, "People need responsibility. They resist assuming it, but they cannot get along without it." Project managers carry a heavy load of responsibilities and to fulfill them they require a combination of administrative, management, analytical, and interpersonal skills. The typical responsibilities of a project man-

24

ager can be divided into two main categories of planning (covering phases 1 and 2) and producing (covering phases 3 and 4) as shown in Figure 1.1.

Responsibilities during planning (Phases 1 and 2):

- *Establish* (with the client) project objectives and success criteria
- *Identify* stakeholders and project requirements
- *Plan* for integration of interfaces and interrelationship of tasks, organization, and hardware
- *Identify* risk areas and develop a risk management strategy
- *Relate* project's contribution towards overall organizational strategy
- *Develop* an integrated Work Breakdown Structure, schedule and budget
- *Assemble* resources from a variety of sources (internal and external).
- *Organize* the team into an integrated whole
- *Delegate* appropriate tasks and ensure project control and adherence to the project plan
- *Communicate* across interfaces; ensure that team members communicate effectively.

Responsibilities during producing (Phases 3 and 4):

- *Execute the plan, solve* problems, and remove roadblocks
- *Direct and influence* the project to assure interfaces are recognized and the tasks are completed and integrated as a "whole"
- *Monitor, review,* and *update* the project plan continually
- *Build team,* establish team norms, team roles and an environment of maximum harmony and minimum conflict
- *Motivate* and *assure* that jobs are organized to provide built-in potential motivators
- *Resolve* conflicts quickly and amicably
- *Set* priorities and *negotiate* trade-offs
- *Forecast* end results
- *Ensure* adequate and timely completion of project records and documentation
- *Identify* training, testing, and commissioning programs to achieve smooth, full operation on schedule.

Project managers generally have increased responsibility, but limited authority. To overcome this limitation, they must negotiate company resources with upper-level management as well as with functional managers. Project managers must also be able to interface effectively with clients, contractors, and other internal and external stakeholders who have a direct or indirect influence on the project's outcome.

Important skills of a project manager

Ability will never catch up with a demand for it.

— *Malcolm S. Forbes*

Today, projects are multi-disciplinary and highly complex. Project managers must be able to manage across functional boundaries and deal effectively with a variety of support personnel over whom they have very little or no formal authority. Project managers also have to manage a variety of interfaces and cope with constant and rapid change of technology, markets, regulations, and socioeconomic factors. Generally, project managers are selected and advanced primarily based on their quantitative skills in areas such as planning, scheduling, cost estimating, financial control, and critical path analysis. However, in today's competitive environment, project managers must also have abilities to manage quality, time-to-market, innovations, subcontractors, technological changes, and clients.[13] Various researchers have found that project management requires expertise and skills in three primary areas:[14,15,16]

- Leadership and interpersonal
- Administrative
- Technical.

Thamhain summarized skills in these areas and prepared a skills inventory of the project manager[13] shown in Table 1.1. To be successful, project managers must understand the tasks, the tools, the people, and the organizations.

Project managers, who are apparently expected to perform miracles, must have a combination of skills to carry them through the whole project management process and successfully meet the project objectives.[17]

Basic management skills. A project manager's performance depends on how well he or she gets activities done by others; therefore, mastery of the various managerial skills is critical.

Technical skills are mostly related to working with processes, tools, or physical objects. They refer to using specialized knowledge and experience related to project management and the specific technology of the project for executing project activities. These skills are necessary to communicate effectively with the project team to assess risks, and to make trade-offs between cost, schedule, and technical issues.[13]

Conceptual skills refer to the ability to see the "big picture." Project managers with good conceptual skills are well aware of how various functions of the organization complement one another. They understand relationships between projects, the overall organization and its environment, and how changes in one part of the organization affect the whole. Conceptual skills are necessary to appropriately deal with project politics and to acquire adequate support from top management.

Human skills build cooperation between the project team, other project stakeholders, and the project manager. Major human skills involve communication, team building, leadership, influencing, understanding perceptions and attitudes, interface management, integration, improving morale of individuals and groups, etc. Human skills are important for all levels of management.

26

Table 1.1 Skills Inventory of a Project Manager

Leadership/ Interpersonal	Project Management/ Administration	Technical
Visionary, credible, action-oriented, self-starter	Planning and organizing multi-functional programs	Technical credibility, understanding of system perspective and "big picture"
Understanding of the organization; ability to manage in an unstructured work environment	Communicating effectively (written, oral) to expedite project communications and work with other organizations	Understanding of technology, market trends, product applications and ability to manage these effectively
Communication (oral, written); provides clear, compelling directions	Estimating and negotiating resources; attracting and holding quality people	Communicating with technical personnel, unifying the technical team and encouraging creativity
Building multi-disciplinary teams and inspiring high team performance through motivation, collaborative problem solving and effective conflict management	Scheduling multi-disciplinary activities and preparing budgets and cash flow	Facilitating trade-offs and assisting in problem solving
Ability to achieve higher visibility and priority; gaining upper management support and commitment	Monitoring and reporting work status, progress, performance and forecasting to completion	Integrating technical, business and human objectives and resources
Sensitivity to personal goals, professional needs and growth opportunities	Understanding of policies, operating procedures, regulations and concerns of external stakeholders	Understanding engineering and technical tools and methods

Successful project managers combine these three skill types. The distribution of each skill type depends upon the positional authority of project manager, project life cycle, size, nature of the project, and its constraints. It is important to achieve a balanced mix of these skills as necessary throughout the project life cycle.

Interpersonal skills. Interpersonal skills form a major component of human skills and can be divided into:

- Motivation and leadership ability (within a project and in the overall organization), and
- Skills in intergroup relationships (communicating, team building, group dynamics, and conflict resolution).

Interpersonal skills require understanding people, their attitudes, and human dynamics. They represent the ability of a project manager to work effectively as a project team leader and to build cooperative effort with the project members and all other groups with which the project team interacts. They are most critical for effective performance in a project environment. Major interpersonal skills include: communication, team building, leadership, coaching, motivating, decision making, delegating, training, directing, persuading/influencing, negotiating, and supporting those involved in the project. Project managers must be sensitive to cultural differences when dealing with different people and their perceptions, values, and attitudes. This is particularly true for international projects consisting of people from diverse cultures. Good interpersonal skills build trust among project team members and help create satisfying relationships and a good working environment. Major interpersonal skills required to manage projects effectively are discussed in Volume 2 of this series.

People can alter their lives by altering their attitudes.

— *William James*

Attitudes represent patterns of feelings, beliefs, values, and behavior tendencies directed towards specific persons, groups, ideas, events, or objects.[18] They result from one's background and life experiences and influence behavior. Three main components of attitude are:[19]

Affective refers to feelings, sentiments, moods, and emotions.

Cognitive refers to the beliefs, values, opinions, knowledge or information held by the individual.

Behavioral refers to the intention and predisposition to act.

However, in reality, attitudes and their effects on behavior can be extremely complex.[20]

Project managers should try to understand the attitudes that project participants hold towards their project tasks. They should be especially aware of attitudes of project team members towards job satisfaction because such attitudes affect performance and working relationships with others. Some individual differences such as internal or external locus of control (the extent to which individuals believe that they can control events affecting them) and cognitive moral development (individual's level of moral judgment) are related to ethical behavior.[21] Project organizations should foster ethical attitudes among project managers and their project team members.

Attitudes influence the personality of individuals. The project manager must understand these attitudes in order to create harmony and team spirit between project stakeholders. Since the common denominator in all aspects of project management is people, the project manager must possess interpersonal skills in order to interface effectively with people in all directions: vertical, horizontal, and lateral.

Interpersonal skills and attitudes are highly interrelated. They are important regardless of the size of the project and the position of the project manager on the corporate ladder. Project managers will have great difficulty in getting project participants to cooperate with them and with each other if they cannot communicate effectively with individuals involved in the project and cannot see other people's points of view.

Guidelines for improving interpersonal skills. Some general guidelines to improve interpersonal skills that must be learned and practiced by all project managers are shown in Table 1.2.

Project managers should remember that their role is not just to command, direct, control, and inspect, but also to take responsibility for leading, motivating, administering, guiding, consulting, and above all *caring* for project team members. Project managers with good interpersonal skills are generally able to resolve project conflicts and even complex problems expeditiously and without rancor because of the cooperation and trust earned from their team members. They are also effective integrators, which is pivotal in managing complexities in today's projects. Good interpersonal relationships in a project involve the development and maintenance of sound working relationships and better understanding and appreciation of the other participants' culture, beliefs and attitudes, which leads to fewer conflicts and frustration. They motivate all project participants to produce their best and help each other win. Look for opportunities to make people feel important.

Integration and interface management skills. Integration and interface management is the essence of effective project management. Senior management should ensure that project managers have complete responsibility for managing all aspects of the project from beginning to end. The project manager's job description usually specifies attributes, skills, and authority. Project managers are responsible for meeting project objectives by coordinating and integrating activities across multiple functional lines. In addition to strong communication and interpersonal skills, they must be familiar with the operations of each line department, and understand technology in terms of its strengths, maturity, and limitations.

Integration and interface management are very important parts of overall project management. *Integration* mainly refers to management coordination to achieve harmony of individual effort toward the accomplishment of group goals. The project manager also integrates project resources (people, materials, equipment, facilities, and information). Because of rapid advances in technology and increased complexity of programs/projects to be managed, there is an increased need for both greater specialization (differentiation) and for tighter coordination (integration).[22]

Interface management consists of identifying, documenting, scheduling, communicating, and monitoring interfaces related to both the product and the project.[23] The problem of overall project/functional interface

Table 1.2 Interpersonal Skills and Their Functions

Interpersonal Skills	Function
Practice tolerance and understanding of the viewpoints, cultures, attitudes, perceptions, and beliefs of others	Increases respect, credibility and ability to influence others
Communicate with honesty and openness, combined with good listening skills	Leads to motivation, cooperation, and better working relationships
Create an atmosphere in which project team members feel free to express their ideas	Fosters creativity and innovation
Assign work by *request* rather than by direct *order*	Helps increase willingness to work
Delegate jobs in terms of *objectives* rather than *procedures*. Delegation involves assigning appropriate responsibility, granting authority, and requiring accountability	Leads to effective delegation, promotes creativity and a sense of ownership
Be committed to increasing each project team member's contribution in terms of intellectual effort, commitment to the project, and quality and quantity of output	Makes each member of the project team a *valued* member
Be more like a *facilitator/coach* than a controller	Increases maturity level of teams and leads to self-directed project teams
Foster a spirit of cooperation and trust between the project manager, project team members, functional managers, and others involved in the project	Leads to true teamwork and human synergy
Take pride in success of others	Enhances trust and motivates the project team
Give proper recognition and rewards for jobs well done	Keeps team morale high
Keep a positive attitude towards your project team members and their ideas	Positive attitude is contagious!

is discussed at some length by Cleland and King,[24] who stressed that project and functional organizations are complementary to each other. They are inseparable and one cannot survive without the other. The project manager is expected to continually monitor personal, organizational, and system interfaces to identify and resolve potential difficulties.[25]

Typically, the project manager has more responsibility than authority, especially over functional resource managers, other departments, and client personnel. Moreover, he or she must negotiate resources between top management and functional management. This role in terms of interface management can be described as:[26]

- Managing human relationships in the project organization
- Maintaining the balance between technical and managerial project functions
- Coping with the risk associated with project management
- Surviving within organizational constraints.

The project manager, as the key person having a comprehensive view of the whole project from its inception to completion, must be able to see potential interface and/or integration conflicts. Project managers must establish a climate of open communication and maintain effective communication links across the organizational interfaces. They must be able to accurately and quickly analyze, evaluate, synthesize, condense, and act on information and ideas from project team members and others involved in the project. They must see themselves as catalysts to motivate the project team and create an environment that nurtures their creativity.

Project managers coordinate internal actions with the external environment (i.e., dealing with public, press, and regulatory personnel). They must interact very closely with the customer/project sponsor, outside consultants, contractors, project team members, project engineer, and other third parties to meet project objectives within the specified constraints.

Negotiating is another important skill critical for integration and for interfacing with all the stakeholders effectively. By this process, parties with differing interests reach agreement through communication and compromise. A straightforward, no-nonsense strategy for pursuing self-interest while recognizing conflicting interests of others is outlined by Fisher and Ury in their book *Getting to Yes: Negotiating Agreement Without Giving In.*[27]

For example, in construction projects, conflicts often arise when dealing with contractors and subcontractors. Effective negotiation emphasizes developing an agreement based on its merits and not on which party wins or loses. It enhances mutual benefit, respect, and project success. Project managers must encourage such negotiation because it leads to future contracts and a profitable relationship between satisfied clients, project managers, and contractors and subcontractors. Identification of major project stakeholders and guidelines for managing them are discussed in greater detail in Chapter 2.

Putting traits, roles and skills together

Project managers are expected to accomplish project objectives by using their knowledge, skills, and practical experience. During the project management process, they have to use a combination of their personal traits/characteristics, typical roles (interpersonal, informational, and decisional) and skills (basic management, interpersonal, and integration/interface management). All these should help them to be effective project managers, which involves acting as:

- Leader (develops and communicates vision, inspires high team performance)
- Entrepreneur (adopts and sells the plan and eventually pushes it to success)
- Manager (carries operational planning and execution by using interface management and integration)
- Administrator (looks after day-to-day details with a compulsion to closure or completeness).

All these roles and characteristics are equally important (in their own right) in managing a project successfully. Successful project managers are expected to and must play any one, or a combination of these roles, depending upon the situation and the phase of the project life cycle (see Figure 1.1).

For example, project managers should place relatively more emphasis on their role as leaders during the concept phase, as entrepreneurs during the development phase, as managers during the execution phase, and as administrators during the finish/termination phase. However, it should be recognized that although these four roles have some of their own distinct characteristics, there are also some characteristics that are common and overlapping. Effective project managers should be able to tailor their roles to the size, complexity, and environment of the project; cultural diversity of the people and overall organizational culture; and the circumstances surrounding the project management issues at hand.

Effective Human Resource Management Model

Project managers must develop appropriate skills for operating in a global and multi-cultural environment. They must develop clear understanding of the human aspects of project management and effective management of project human resources. A combination and a balanced mix of basic management, project management, and interpersonal and leadership skills are required to meet project objectives. Figure 1.2 shows a model for effectively managing project human resources and inspiring high team performance, which consists of four key factors:

- Communication
- Teamwork
- Leadership
- Cultural ambiance.

32

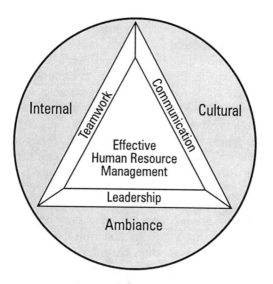

Figure 1.2 Model for Effective Human Resource Management

Internal

Cultural

Teamwork

Communication

Effective
Human Resource
Management

Leadership

Ambiance

Cultural ambiance impacts overall human resource management, as well as influencing Teamwork, Leadership, and Communication.

Hence, effective Project Human Resource Management is a function of Teamwork, Leadership, Communication and Cultural Ambiance.

This is the essence of project management integration.

Communication, teamwork, and leadership are vital components of effective management of project human resources. These incorporate all major skills required to accomplish project objectives successfully. They are all interrelated and critical to project success. Project management faces greater challenges due to increased need for joint ventures and international projects characterized by cultural diversity in project teams and stakeholders. Cultural ambiance plays a significant role by itself in dealing with people and also influences communications, teamwork, and leadership in a project environment. Project managers must develop appropriate organizational designs and project management strategies to facilitate open communication, effective teamwork, and a leadership style that inspires high performance of all project participants throughout the project life cycle.

Communication

Communication provides the wings for flight to success.

Communication is a vital element of project human resource management. A project manager uses communication more than any other skill set in the project management process to ensure that team members work cohesively on the project and resolve their mutual problems effectively. Successful project leaders rely heavily upon their ability to communicate vision and inspire project participants towards high performance.

Communication can be defined as a process by which information is exchanged between individuals through a common system of symbols, signs, or behavior.[28] In project management, the importance of communication is emphasized by Sievert, who says "A high percentage of the frictions, frustrations, and inefficiencies in working relationships are traceable to poor communication."[29] In almost every case, the misinterpretation of a design drawing, a misunderstood change order, a missed delivery date, or a failure to execute instructions result from a breakdown in communication.

Communications can make or break the project. Project managers must establish appropriate communication channels and design project organizational structures that facilitate open and effective communication and foster creativity, real team spirit, and human synergy.

Effective listening is perhaps the most important component of communication. It is a skill that some project managers, selected primarily on the basis of their technical and quantitative skills, may lack. To become a good listener, project managers study good listening practices and apply them in a conscious program of self-development. Alliances with major stakeholders can only be built and maintained through active listening and opening up communication channels to keep messages flowing in both directions. In addition to improving project communications, this usually facilitates the development of mutual trust, respect, and good working relationships, enhancing overall team performance.

Davis[30] has commented on the role of communication and its relationship to management style in encouraging frankness and integrity in the management of a project. Project managers are challenged by communication issues due to overlapping areas of responsibility, lack of authority, delegation problems, inappropriate organizational structures, and conflicts with and among various project participants.

While communicating with project team members and other project stakeholders, project managers should avoid *negative* and *absolute* statements in favor of positive, collaborative, or open-ended statements.[31] (See Table 1.3.)

Communication is complex. Yet since competent communication leads to effective leadership, interface management, integration, and high team performance, project managers must work at removing communication

34

Table 1.3 Common Statements and Their Impacts

Statement	Impact
"Why don't you..."	Negative
"What if we..."	Positive
"I hate it when... "	Negative
"Wouldn't it be better if..."	Positive
"John always says that..."	Absolute
"I have heard John say that..."	Nonabsolute
"Nothing of good quality gets done around here."	Absolute
"Sometimes we've had problems getting good quality work done here."	Nonabsolute
"We must do it this way."	Absolute
"Here is an idea worth considering..."	Nonabsolute

barriers (caused by themselves or by other project personnel) to achieve effective project communications throughout the project life cycle.

Teamwork

If everyone is moving forward together, then success takes care of itself.

Dramatic increases in project complexity require individuals with a diverse mix of backgrounds, skills, and expertise to be integrated into an effective unit—a project team. In a team environment, people work *interdependently* rather than *independently*. Increasingly, stringent project performance requirements mandate a high level of sustained cooperative effort within the project team. Project managers must recognize the critical significance of the effective project team and the role of team building in facilitating this high performance standard.

Project managers must understand interpersonal and group dynamics to optimize productivity at the individual as well as at the team level. While belonging to a successful project team is very satisfying, creating such a team is equally rewarding for the project manager. Beyond that, project managers must continue to provide routine care and feeding of team members.

The working relationships among the project team members affect not only their individual or team productivity, but also affect their performance in relation to the client and the support groups. Therefore, teamwork is a critical factor for project success, and developing effective project teams is one of the prime responsibilities of the project manager. Team development involves a whole spectrum of project management skills to identify, commit, and integrate the project participants from traditional functional organizations into multi-disciplinary and highly cohesive project teams.

Project managers must create an environment that facilitates real teamwork and fosters human synergy. They must acquire skills to identify, build, maintain, motivate, lead, and inspire project teams to achieve high team performance and to meet or exceed the project's objectives. They must understand the issues associated with teams in the project environment, such as the importance of team building, the team building process, and the major tasks in building project teams to suit the various phases of the project life cycle. The drivers and barriers to high team performance must be identified and solutions developed to minimize the negative impact of these barriers. Project managers should continually motivate their team by providing challenges and opportunities, by providing support as needed, and by recognizing the team members for good performance. High team performance can be inspired and real teamwork achieved by using open and effective communication, developing trust among team members, managing conflicts in a constructive manner, and encouraging collaborative problem-solving and participative decision making.

Leadership

Success comes to those who make it happen, not to those who let it happen.
— Anonymous

Effective teamwork is the by-product of good leadership. During my workshop presentations one participant made the point, "There is nothing worse than being on a team where communication is not open, no one trusts anyone else, and there is no team leadership."

There is an ample body of literature on communication, teamwork, and leadership. However, it is still not very clear what project leadership is and how it relates to project management. Verma and Wideman dealt with this issue in addressing the question, *Is it leadership or management that is most needed for managing projects successfully in the next century?*[32]

About project leadership. There has been a spate of publications on leadership and team building by authors such as Batten, Bennis, Covey, Depree, Dilenschneider, McLean, Fisher, and others.[33] Most of these authors agree that vision is a primary ingredient of leadership. Batten defines leadership as "development of a clear and complete system of expectations in order to identify, evoke, and use the strengths of all resources in the organization, the most important of which is people."[34] John Naisbit probably comes closer to a definition of a leader with his description: "An ability to attract followers ... a clear destination, and ... a timetable."[35] With these attributes in mind, leadership in a project context can be defined in the following simple, yet comprehensive, distillation of leadership thought.

Project leadership is an ability to get things done well through others. It requires:

- A vision of the destination *(project goal)*
- A clear, compelling reason to get there *(to inspire commitment)*
- A set of directions and a realistic timetable *(project plan covering schedules, budget, etc.)*
- A capacity to attract a willing team and make it work *(developing and fostering teamwork).*

Pinto synthesized various leadership studies and indicated the following points about the nature of project leadership:

- Effective project leaders must be good communicators.
- Project leaders are flexible in responding to ambiguous or uncertain situations with a minimum of stress.
- Successful project leaders work well with and through their project team.
- Good project leaders are skilled at various influence tactics by using the art of persuasion and influence.

He pointed out that examining the traits of successful leaders is valuable but not sufficient. One key to understanding leadership behavior is to focus on what leaders *do* rather than on who they are.[36]

Verma and Wideman[32] raised two interesting issues and questions about leadership in a project environment.

Leader versus manager. Is there a difference between a project leader and a project manager? Careful analysis of the roles of project managers and project leaders reveals that the distinction between their styles can be attributed to how and what they focus on. Leaders focus on "doing the right things" (effectiveness) while managers focus on "doing the things right" (efficiency). The respective positions of leaders and managers on a number of issues are shown in Table 1.4.[33]

Successful project management requires both project leadership and project management skills. Collectively project leadership and project managership may be called project *stewardship,* which implies holding something in trust for another. Project stewardship refers to a willingness to be fully accountable for meeting project objectives and for giving a higher degree of importance to project objectives than to self-interest. It entails holding people accountable without harshly exacting compliance from them.

Leadership and the project life cycle. Do project leaders need different skills and leadership styles in different phases of the project life cycle? Both project leadership and managership are important to project success. Leadership emphasizes communicating the vision and then motivating and inspiring project participants to higher performance, whereas managership focuses on getting things done. Can the two be reconciled? To answer this, it is essential to turn to a fundamental principle of project management.

Table 1.4 Leader or Manager?

Leaders Focus On:	Managers Focus On:
Vision	Objectives
Selling what and why	Telling how and when
Longer range	Shorter range
People	Organization and structure
Democracy	Autocracy
Enabling	Restraining
Developing	Maintaining
Challenging	Conforming
Originating	Imitating
Innovating	Administrating
Directing	Controlling
Policy	Procedures
Flexibility	Consistency
Risk (opportunity)	Risk (avoidance)
Top line	Bottom line
Good Leaders *do the right things*	**Good Managers** *do things right*

Project management is a structured but flexible process, producing a new end result (a unique product or service). Its success depends upon the successful application of a two-step process: first *plan* and then *produce*. This is the genesis of a typical project life cycle. Figure 1.3 shows these phases, along with the leadership versus managership skills needed during various phases of the project life cycle.[32]

For example, in the planning phases, the project leader focuses on the "right things to do" and outlines strategies to achieve agreed-upon objectives. This challenging process requires teamwork by all project stakeholders. It may be an iterative process and therefore takes time. During the planning phases the customer's needs, requirements, and expectations should be clearly fleshed out. Therefore visioning, intelligence gathering, and developing a compelling reason and appropriate strategies are all important issues in these phases. The process in these phases also forms the essential basis for effective team development.

On the other hand, the real work of project execution gets done in the production phases. In these phases, the emphasis is on "getting things done" by combining the efforts of the project team. At the same time, it is

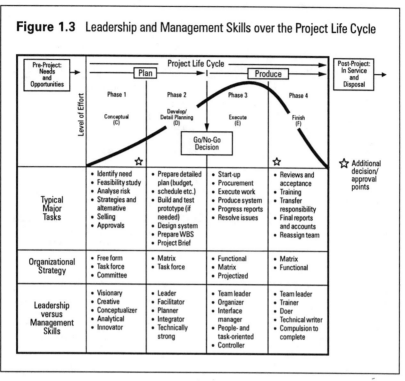

Figure 1.3 Leadership and Management Skills over the Project Life Cycle

	Phase 1 Conceptual (C)	Phase 2 Develop/ Detail Planning (D)	Phase 3 Execute (E)	Phase 4 Finish (F)
Typical Major Tasks	• Identify need • Feasibility study • Analyse risk • Strategies and alternative • Selling • Approvals	• Prepare detailed plan (budget, schedule etc.) • Build and test prototype (if needed) • Design system • Prepare WBS • Project Brief	• Start-up • Procurement • Execute work • Produce system • Progress reports • Resolve issues	• Reviews and acceptance • Training • Transfer responsibility • Final reports and accounts • Reassign team
Organizational Strategy	• Free form • Task force • Committee	• Matrix • Task force	• Functional • Matrix • Projectized	• Matrix • Functional
Leadership versus Management Skills	• Visionary • Creative • Conceptualizer • Analytical • Innovator	• Leader • Facilitator • Planner • Integrator • Technically strong	• Team leader • Organizer • Interface manager • People- and task-oriented • Controller	• Team leader • Trainer • Doer • Technical writer • Compulsion to complete

Pre-Project: Needs and Opportunities → Project Life Cycle (Plan → Produce) → Post-Project: In Service and Disposal

Go/No-Go Decision

☆ Additional decision/approval points

Source: Vijay K. Verma and R. Max Wideman. 1994. Project Manager to Project Leader? and the Rocky Road Between. *Proceedings of the 25th Annual Seminar/Symposium of the Project Management Institute.* Upper Darby, PA:Project Management Institute, pp. 627–633.

important to focus on "doing the things right," i.e., efficiency, to satisfy the requirements of the client within the specified constraints.

As shown in the project life cycle in Figure 1.3, in the planning phase (phases 1 and 2), *managership*, as described above, has its limitations and *leadership* skills are more appropriate. On the other hand, during the production phase (phases 3 and 4), *leadership* has its limitations and *managership* is more effective.

Thus, project success depends upon a combination of both project leadership and project managership. To get a project launched on the right foot, the project manager must become a leader. The style or major emphasis of leadership changes as the project progresses through its life cycle. For example, it is essential to place more emphasis on project managership towards the end of the project, when efficient project administration and a compulsion for closure help to integrate and realign everyone's efforts and transfer the product to the client. Figure 1.4 shows the relationship between different phases of the project in its life cycle, leadership style, and the skills and factors which should be emphasized to achieve project success.

Figure 1.4 Leadership and the Project Life Cycle

Phase	Major Attributes/Emphasis	Leadership Style/Blend
Feasibility Study (Pre-formulation)	• Sense of vision • Conceptual, sees "Big Picture" • Analytical	• Visionary • Creates future • Empowerment • Expansive
Conceptual (Formulation)	• Listening • Analysis • Alignment	• Analytical • Listener • Change master • Convergence
Development	• Participative/acceptance and commitment • Cooperative	• Team builder • Power and influence • Integrator
Execution	• Re-alignment	• Decision-maker • Balances work and fun • Trustworthiness • Team and synergy
Completion	• Transfer of product and information	• Administrator • Closure

Source: Vijay K. Verma and R. Max Wideman. 1994. Project Manager to Project Leader? and the Rocky Road Between. *Proceedings of the 25th Annual Seminar/Symposium of the Project Management Institute.* Upper Darby, PA: Project Management Institute, pp. 627-633.

Cultural Ambiance

We are a community of learners. Be alert to opportunities to learn from people of diverse cultures.

As we move into the 21st century, project management faces major challenges because of increased global competition and greater complexity in project organizations. The increased need for joint ventures and international projects leads to increased cultural diversity among project team members and other major stakeholders. Project managers operating in international settings must develop appropriate project management styles and strategies.

Management of both domestic and international projects requires effective planning, organizing, and controlling. However, management of international projects and joint ventures poses additional human resource management challenges related to communication, teamwork, and leadership, as a result of the diverse cultural backgrounds of the project participants. This presents interesting challenges in negotiation, motivation, and human relations.

Project managers must understand the major elements of culture, including material culture, language, aesthetics, education, religious beliefs and attitudes, social organizations, and political life.[37] Figure 1.5 shows

Organizing Projects for Success

Figure 1.5 Major Cultural Elements Affecting Projects

Cultural Element	What It Means or Implies	Impact on Project	Recommendations/ Comments
Material Culture	• Refers to tools, skills, work habits and work attitudes	• Determines technical and manpower constraints	• This formation is needed for planning and negotiations
Language	• Medium of communication • Words and experiences may differ	• Affects communications • Influences understanding of beliefs and values	• Learning foreign language develops better understanding and rapport
Aesthetics	• Arts, music, dance, traditions and customs	• Encourages informal and open communication • Influences success directly	• Relationships are enriched by encouraging informal communication
Education	• Transmission of knowledge through learning process • Approach to problems and people	• Affects project planning and negotiations	• Knowledge of education system helps in determining level of skills and expertise (helpful in project planning and negotiations)
Religion, Beliefs and Attitudes	• Mainspring of culture • Affects dress, eating habits, attitudes of workers towards work, punctuality and work site	• Emphasizes on promptness and punctuality	• Appreciation of religion, beliefs and values develops mutual trust, respects and improves cooperation and team spirit
Social Organization	• Organizations/groups (labor unions, social clubs) • Relate to social classes	• Influences formal/informal communication • Affects business contacts for negotiating	• Social skills can lead to better results than formal meetings
Political Life	• Government involvement in joint ventures with foreign companies • Concerned about treatment of people, jobs, financial, economic and safety factors	• Affects delivery of materials, supplies and equipment • Influences permits and licenses	• Staying in tune with political life helps identify the strengths, constraints and business contacts

Adapted from: M. Dean Martin. 1981. The Negotiation Differential for International Project Management. *Proceedings of the Annual Seminar/Symposium of the Project Management Institute.* Drexel Hill, PA: Project Management Institute pp. 450–453.

these cultural elements, their meaning, and their impacts on projects. Project managers must identify and understand the critical dimensions of cultural differences when dealing with people. These dimensions include power distance (dealing with inequality and degree of dependence in relationships); individualistic/collectivistic; masculinity/femininity; uncertainty avoidance (tolerance for ambiguity and uncertainty within the workplace); and time horizon (long-term and short-term plans).[38] Project managers working on projects characterized by cultural diversity must appreciate these cultural differences and try to increase team effectiveness by fostering cultural synergy within their project team.

Currency fluctuations, political instability, competitors from national and regional governments, and special interest groups can interfere in the management process of international projects. Project managers must consider special attributes of international projects which include project plans, communication and information systems, control systems, team building and team ethics, leadership and followership issues, project management training and techniques, and human subsystems (motivation, communication, negotiations, and conflict management).[39] The primary factors in cross-cultural settings should be recognized and appropriate strategies should be developed to manage communication, teamwork, human resources, risk and contract management.[40]

Cultural ambiance affects the management of human resources because of different perceptions about work, project management, and human relations. Among the characteristics and skills needed to get ahead, communication is the most important. This includes speaking, writing, listening, and reading ability, followed by the ability to be a good team player, team leader, problem solver, and decision maker.

EFFECTIVE MANAGEMENT OF HUMAN RESOURCES—the most valuable assets and resources in a project—can be achieved if project managers evaluate and use all four factors (communication, teamwork, leadership, and cultural ambiance) to build an effective intercultural team and integrate the efforts of a diverse mix of team members. They must recognize that change is inevitable and therefore focus on developing appropriate project management strategies to convert change into opportunity by optimizing the performance of all human resources in a project.

Regarding the rapid rate of change and the necessity to be fully prepared to manage it, Northern Telecom's David Vice was quoted in the prologue to Tom Peters' book *Liberation Management* as saying: "The nineties will be a decade in a hurry, a nanosecond culture. There will only be two kinds of managers: the quick and the dead."[41]

Summary

Projects are basic building blocks for developing industrial and business organizations. "Management by projects" is becoming the competitive way to manage organizations. Most projects are characterized by the need to meet a set of objectives given limited resources and time constraints. Project management is the art of directing and coordinating human and material resources to meet these project objectives.

All projects are done by people and therefore project human resource management is the most important component of project management. Most project managers agree that the majority of project problems are of a behavioral nature rather than a technical nature.

Project managers must manage people, organizational, and systems interfaces. The project management process must integrate both sets of project management functions: management of constraints (scope, quality, time, and costs); and management of interactive/facilitative functions (management of communications, contract/procurement, risk, and human resources) to satisfy all project stakeholders. All projects progress through a life cycle of four phases: conception, development, execution, and completion. Each phase is marked by deliverables that feed into the subsequent phase. The type of expertise needed on the project and the organizational design strategies should be adjusted according to the phase of the project life cycle.

The project manager is like a conductor of an orchestra who must ensure that all team members work together in harmony. This requires special people skills. Successful project managers are high achievers, committed to playing their roles effectively and to fulfilling all responsibilities to meet project objectives. The important skills of a successful project manager include: basic management skills (balanced mix of technical, conceptual, and human skills); interpersonal skills (motivation, leadership, conflict resolution, negotiation, persuasion/influence etc.); and integration and interface management skills.

A high proportion of project problems are caused by some kind of communication breakdown including lack of active listening; uncohesive teams; uncoordinated teamwork; and poor project leadership. General project management faces additional challenges due to the increased need for joint ventures. Moreover, international projects are characterized by the cultural diversity of the project teams and the project stakeholders. These factors emphasize the need to manage project human resources effectively through the understanding and use of a model that includes three elements: teamwork(T), leadership(L), and communication(C), otherwise known as TLC (tender loving care).

Therefore, it is essential to understand the major elements of culture and critical dimensions of cultural differences when dealing with people in managing projects. In order to achieve human synergy and inspire high performance among all the people working on the project, appropriate strategies and skills must be used to facilitate communication, foster teamwork, and provide effective leadership.

chapter

2

Outline

Organizing Projects for Success

Be wiser than other people if you can, but do not tell them so.
— Anonymous

2

Interfacing with the Major Stakeholders

P ROJECTS ARE LIKE team sports: all participants play a vital role. Project participants, who may have a diverse mix of backgrounds, interests, and skills, must work together harmoniously and contribute to each other's effectiveness if project goals are to be met successfully. Project managers must interact with a number of project stakeholders, those key individuals or groups who have an interest in the outcome of the project and who are directly or indirectly associated with it.

Project stakeholders play a significant role in the project management process throughout the project life cycle. There are many different categories of project stakeholders and each of them may have different objectives. To manage the project stakeholders successfully, it is important to identify them, recognize their roles, their main interests, and the relationships between them and with other stakeholders.

Project managers must identify major stakeholders (internal and external) and earn their cooperation and trust to meet project objectives successfully. They must develop and use a balanced mix of conceptual, technical, and human skills, with special emphasis on effective management of human resources. This can be achieved through a practical understanding and application of three key factors—teamwork, communication, and leadership—along with an appreciation for the impact of cultural ambiance. These factors enhance trust and creativity and inspire high team performance among all project stakeholders.

Successful analysis and management of project stakeholders leads to effective project integration and utilization of planning and control systems throughout the project life cycle. ■

Identifying and Classifying the Major Stakeholders

The success of the journey of project management depends upon the relationships with fellow passengers.

— Anonymous

Project management involves a great deal of integration and interface management. Project managers wear several different hats and assume several different roles. They must interact with a number of stakeholders who are directly or indirectly associated with the project. They must interface effectively with all project stakeholders and earn their cooperation and trust in order to create a true team environment where everyone helps to optimize each other's contributions towards meeting project objectives.

Project stakeholders play a pivotal role in the management process and its outcome. In general, the project stakeholders are defined as those who are:
• Directly or indirectly associated with the project
• Affected in the long/short term by the project and its activities
• Interested in the outcome of the project.

There are many different names and categories of internal and external project stakeholders: clients and sponsors; contractors/subcontractors and suppliers; owners and operators; project team members and their families; competitors and special interest groups; bankers and creditors; government regulatory, protection and legal agencies; the public, the press, and society at large. Sometimes it is not easy to differentiate clearly between these categories and between project participants and stakeholders, because of an overlap in their roles, interests, and concerns. The naming or grouping of stakeholders can help identify which individuals and organizations see themselves as stakeholders.

Interfacing with and managing stakeholders is a vital element of project management. For strategic management of any organization, it is important to analyze the environment and the stakeholders in order to formulate and implement the organization's strategies.[1,2,3] Managing stakeholder expectations is challenging because stakeholders have different objectives and concerns. As a first step, it is important to identify the probable stakeholders of the project and then determine how they are likely to react to project goals and decisions, what influence their reactions will carry, and how they might interact with each other and the project team to affect the chances for success.[4] Several authors have presented strategies to deal with stakeholders in a corporation.[5,6,7,8,9]

Project stakeholders form a vital element of the project environment. For successful management of any program or project, it is important to define the general and the operating environment (as shown in Figure 2.1) and identify all potential stakeholders who are directly or indirectly interested in the project outcome. Their relative ability to influence should be determined and an appropriate project environment created in order to facilitate effective interfacing between the project managers and

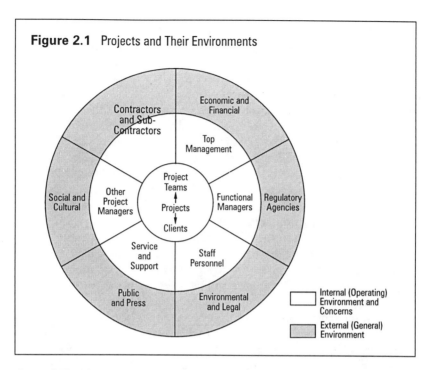

Figure 2.1 Projects and Their Environments

Contractors and Sub-Contractors

Economic and Financial

Top Management

Social and Cultural

Other Project Managers

Project Teams
↑
Projects
↓
Clients

Functional Managers

Regulatory Agencies

Service and Support

Staff Personnel

Public and Press

Environmental and Legal

☐ Internal (Operating) Environment and Concerns

▨ External (General) Environment

the stakeholders. Stakeholders may be classified in any of several categories or groupings:[10,11]

- *Clients or Project Sponsor:* The ultimate users of outputs and results of the project. They may include customer, clients, project sponsor, or project owners (within the organization).

- *Internal Stakeholders:* Those who are directly related to the project, such as suppliers of inputs. They create an operating environment for the project and primarily include members of the home organization. They may include top management, functional managers, project engineers, staff personnel, service and support personnel, and other project managers.

- *External Stakeholders:* These include stakeholders who are indirectly involved with the project and have indirect external influence on the physical, infrastructural, technological, financial, economic, political, or legal conditions associated with the project. They may also include regulatory authorities, environmental protection agencies, and other government authorities at local, regional, and national level. They create a general external environment that should be analyzed by the project manager to capitalize on positive factors and minimize the impact of negative factors.

- *Contractors and Subcontractors:* These can be classified as internal or external stakeholders, depending upon their degree of involvement.

Sometimes, they may be active project participants and become members of the project team itself. In other cases, they may supply key components and/or be brought in for specific assignments or for some kind of independent review of the project, its tasks, or organizational strategies.

- *Project Team:* Project teams members are involved in either the technical aspects of the project or in project management and administration. Team members usually work directly with or under the project manager, depending upon how the project is organized. Team members who are involved in the technical aspects of the project mainly focus on doing the project tasks and activities (as outlined in different phases of the project life cycle), which may include engineering, procurement, construction, testing, documentation, etc. Team members who are involved in the project management and administration process provide project management services, which typically include planning, scheduling, budgeting, collecting and disseminating information, contract administration, coordinating, interfacing, integration, preparing status reports, and tracking the overall project in terms of budget, schedule, and quality.

  Some project team members may be involved in both the technical aspects and project management aspects while others may specialize in a specific area. Teamwork is vital to project success and project managers must develop and use team building skills to inspire high team performance. The concepts and practical guidelines for developing and sustaining the project team and the behavioral issues associated with project team members and project teams themselves are covered in Volume 3 of this series.

- *Competitors and Others:* Individuals, groups, and associations who have vested interests and may or may not be related to the project. In the case of competitors and special interest groups, they may see the project as an opportunity to pursue their own interests.

Having identified the various stakeholders and classified them in categories, project managers should recognize their roles and their relative ability to influence the project outcome. Each of the above categories of stakeholders should be elaborated in detail by identifying the type of personnel or groups in each category with which the project manager must interface. The roles of these players and how they affect project success are described in subsequent sections of this chapter.

A successful project manager should try to influence the project's operating environment by developing the attitude of *we care* and by fostering the commitment of project stakeholders. This attitude is best attained by changing the "responsive up" philosophy to a "service" mindset inverting the traditional management hierarchy (Figure 2.2). With this

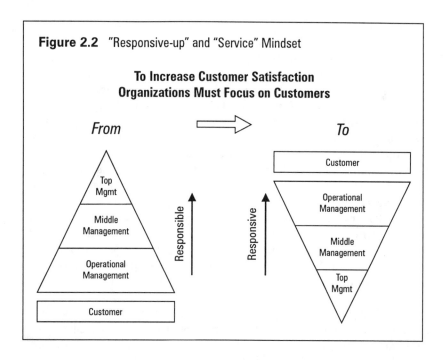

Figure 2.2 "Responsive-up" and "Service" Mindset

**To Increase Customer Satisfaction
Organizations Must Focus on Customers**

mindset the project team can better fulfill its role of optimizing the project outcome, both in perception and in reality.[11]

Interfacing with the Client, Customer or Owner

A customer is the most important visitor on our premises. He is not dependent on us—we are dependent on him. He is not an outsider in our business—he is a part of it. We are not doing him a favor by serving him—he is doing us a favor by giving us the opportunity to do so.

It costs six times more to attract a new customer than it does to keep an old one.

Of those customers who quit, 68% do so because of an attitude of indifference by the company or a specific individual.

In summary, all these facts say …"Customer Satisfaction Equals Success"

— Source unknown

The interface between the project manager and the client is the most important one in the project. The project client (also sometimes referred to as *the customer* or *the owner* of the project) can be an individual(s) or the representative of an organization for whom the project is undertaken. The client is responsible for defining the project objectives in terms of its deliverables and for providing the financial resources to meet those objectives. Clients are very interested in the final outcome or results of projects because they may either use the results themselves or pass them on to the final user for whom they may have initiated the project.

Project objectives consist of the following three elements:[12]
- Attribute (project completion)
- Yardstick (calendar time line)
- Goal (a specific date).

For internal projects, clients from the parent organization are often called project sponsors. A sponsor takes on the responsibility of defining objectives and providing financial resources. Sponsors may initiate projects for their own departments or parent organization, such as projects to develop financial management information systems, inventory control, human resource management, etc. Sometimes project sponsors initiate a project for an outside customer, in which case they act as main liaisons and drivers to get the projects done within scope, cost, time, and quality constraints. Practically, project sponsors should be members of the senior management team with sufficient organizational authority to carry out their duties, since they are responsible for the final project deliverables. They must be in a position to provide sufficient management support and adequate political shield (as necessary) for the project managers to overcome any obstacles to meeting project objectives.

The client for whom the project is undertaken is not always a single person but may be multiple individuals. The project may be undertaken for a third-party client, such as a government department (departments of defense, highways, public works, etc.), a utility company (hydro or telephone), or manufacturing firm, or it may be undertaken for a department or group within an operating organization. In any case, it must be emphasized that the client/owner or the project sponsor carries ultimate financial authority and controls the project budget. They engage a project manager (as shown in Figure 2.3) to ensure that the project objectives are all met within scope, time, cost, and quality constraints.[13] The client/owner is the ultimate boss who pays the bills; therefore the project manager should make satisfying the client a high priority. To avoid any confusion, "client" will be used in this chapter to represent a customer (owner) or a project sponsor.

Key features of project manager and client interface

When interfacing with the client, the project manager must recognize that the whole project organization should try to satisfy the owner by delivering the project results and outcome within time, cost, and performance constraints. Remember the golden rule: "The one who has the gold makes the rules!"

The client can significantly influence the project management process and its implementation. The amount of support provided by clients depends upon the degree to which they are personally involved in the planning and implementation phases of the project.[14] They should be consulted during the first phase of a program or a project.[15] Consultation with the client at the project's front end is most important because a large

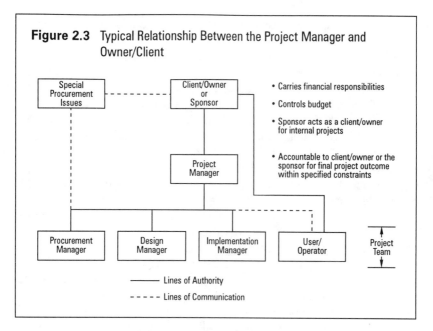

Figure 2.3 Typical Relationship Between the Project Manager and Owner/Client

- Carries financial responsibilities
- Controls budget
- Sponsor acts as a client/owner for internal projects
- Accountable to client/owner or the sponsor for final project outcome within specified constraints

——— Lines of Authority
- - - - - Lines of Communication

percentage of budget is normally committed during the initial phases of the project even though only a small portion is spent at this time.[16]

Client consultation

The project manager should involve and consult the project's sponsor, owner, or other client representatives right at the outset and follow this practice throughout the project life cycle. This is a key to project success. It helps gain their support and commitment and consequently their acceptance upon completion. Important areas for client consultation include:

- Project objectives
- Scope of work with overall schedule, budget and performance specifications
- Project charter and organization
- Responsibility chart and communication links
- Project reporting and tracking techniques
- Sign-off procedures
- Schedule and terms of payment
- Warranties and maintenance.

This list covers the most important areas. However, some items may be added or deleted depending upon the nature of the project and the relationship between the project manager and the client.

Reporting to client/project sponsor

There are several different methods of reporting project progress.[17] The method should be chosen to satisfy the intended audience. For example,

---

upper-level management may be interested in cost and integration of major activities and a summary report will generally be sufficient. For the client, cost and performance data should be included with schedule status and the scheduling technique chosen should be able to answer "what if" questions.

The presentation of schedule, cost, and performance data is both a science and an art. It is a science in the sense that the figures and graphs should be described in understandable symbols and expressions. It is also an art because the diagrams should readily convey the intended message to suit the recipients. For example, in R&D organizations, project participants prefer to see time-scaled logic diagrams or networks, showing relationships between activities, rather than just bar charts or a list of activities with codes, which are traditionally used in a manufacturing environment.

The communication skill of the project manager is the key to successful project management in all environments. Program review meetings, technical discussions, customer summary meetings, and in-house management control meetings all require different forms in terms of techniques, frequency and degree of detail. Effective reporting and control is one of the major components of a creative project management system.[18] Its main purpose should be to inform the project people and provide timely feedback to the project team, which will help in identifying and resolving problem areas before they become serious. Furthermore, every project manager should consider custom tailoring (if necessary) the reporting and control systems to suit the requirements of the client, even if these requirements may vary during different phases of the project.

Generally, clients should interface with projects more closely at the initiation and conceptual planning phase and not interfere during the implementation phase unless required to resolve conflicts or set priorities. However, they may end up "meddling" during the project execution phase if they feel they are not getting accurate information from the project manager.[19] Therefore, project managers must provide sufficient information in order to minimize interference from client representatives and achieve optimum productivity.

General role of the client
Though the project manager's role may be well-defined in the project charter, it still may be perceived differently by the various parties to the project.[15, 20]

If the clients or sponsors are reticent, they may leave it to the project manager to take the initiative in calling meetings to discuss critical technical issues, policies, concerns about schedule, budget, performance, etc. On the other hand, if the clients are aggressive, technically knowledgeable, and like to take a hands-on approach, a more participative climate may be necessary and the project manager should hold extensive discussions before making major decisions.

Organizing Projects for Success

Managerial skills needed to interface with clients

Success in interfacing with the client's representatives, and hence in managing the project, depends a great deal on the technical, human, and conceptual skills of the project manager. Some of the major human skills that a project manager must have in this regard include: communication, motivation, interpersonal, negotiation, problem-solving, conflict resolution, and leadership.

Knowledge of project management techniques and the ability to use this knowledge in interfacing with clients by using some or all of these human skills plays an important role in managing large and complex projects successfully.

Client acceptance

This refers to the final stage in the implementation process when the performance of the project deliverables is determined. Few project managers feel overconfident that clients (whether internal or external) will readily accept the project results just because the earlier stages of the implementation process were accepted. Actually, client acceptance of the project results is a touchy stage, and should be managed very carefully, like a small sub-project.[21]

Some strategies emphasize the importance of client participation in identifying focus areas at the early stages of project planning development to help gain client acceptance of the project results later.[22] "Intermediaries" or "agents" of the client can be used as a liaison between the designer or implementation team and the potential users of the project to ensure smooth transfer to the customer and gain client acceptance.[23] The key to customer acceptance is continuous and open communication, focusing on critical areas and on resolving conflicts and discrepancies as early as possible.

In some cases, top management may sponsor internal or external projects and provide continuous assistance to the project manager and project team. When top management or executives act in this capacity, they assume the role of a project sponsor.

Normally, project success is dependent upon the ability of the project manager to reconcile project constraints of scope, quality, time, and cost in such a way that the customer or project sponsor and all of the participants in the project are satisfied. Project managers should try to get the client on their side and emphasize the importance of working together as a team to create a win-win situation. They must achieve active participation and hence support and commitment from the client. They must build mutual trust, respect, and confidence by genuinely following the objective of serving and satisfying the client. This not only helps in meeting the project objectives within budget, schedule, and performance constraints but also creates a better working relationship, leading to more future business.

Interfacing with Internal Stakeholders (Members of the Home Organization)

Cooperation is spelled with two letters — WE

— Anonymous

The project's internal stakeholders are the various individuals and groups who belong to the home/parent organization. Most are permanent long-term members of the organization, whereas the project manager and project team members may be transient. Internal stakeholders are normally responsible for keeping the primary project functions operating effectively. Project managers deal with these people on a continuous basis. Project success is dependent upon the degree of cooperation, trust, and confidence that project managers get from members of their home organization. Project managers should try to influence the operating environment of their projects for the benefit of all internal stakeholders.[24] They should recognize the importance of all stakeholders and interface with them appropriately both to enrich their project management experiences, as well as to meet the project objectives effectively. The main internal stakeholders, as shown in Figure 2.4, are listed below.

Top management

Top management obviously plays an important role in the project environment. For large projects, top management might simply play the role of directing the activities of a project management services group in their own organization. On the other hand, on not-for-profit projects, political projects, or internal projects in research and development and pharmaceutical industries, top management may very well be the sponsor of the project. In most cases, top management along with the project manager are the vital links with the client. The project manager normally reports to top management about project matters, such as overall schedule, budget, quality management, opportunities, and constraints. Sometimes top management plays the role of the project sponsor in interfacing and integration. In general terms, top management must:

- Establish goals for the company and how these relate to the projects being sponsored
- Establish goals for the project manager
- Provide guidance and support to meet project objectives with respect to schedule, cost, and quality constraints.

Top management may have some particular management styles and philosophies. The role of top management in a project and some associated interfacing issues are described below.

Role of top management in a project. Project managers and their teams must solicit and maintain the support and commitment of top management or project sponsor/executive right from the beginning. They must also try to understand the management style, background, needs, and

54

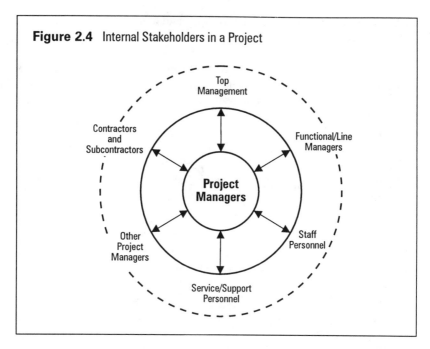

Figure 2.4 Internal Stakeholders in a Project

Top Management

Contractors and Subcontractors

Functional/Line Managers

Project Managers

Other Project Managers

Staff Personnel

Service/Support Personnel

probable reactions of top management. The work environment of the project must fit with the overall organizational mission and culture. The interfacing role of top management is to participate in the following activities:[25]

- In project planning and objective setting
- In conflict resolution
- In priority-setting
- As project sponsor (for internal projects).

Sometimes, when the project is critical to the survival of the organization, top management tends to take over as project manager. This is probably not a good long-term strategy, as top management has too many distractions and generally cannot sustain the effort as project manager.

Working with top management. Project managers and line managers must work together as a team to meet project objectives. The top management must provide advice and guidance to the project manager and provide encouragement to line managers to keep their commitments to the project manager.[25] Top management may sponsor internal or external projects and provide behind-the-scenes assistance to the project manager and project team. With a strong project manager, projects can still be successful without full support and commitment from top management. However, having them as a sounding board and an ally is vital in crisis. This is especially true for complex R&D projects where the project outcome is intangible, uncertain, and requires a long lead time.

Owners or clients feel very comfortable and confident if they can clearly see full support and commitment of top management behind their project. Top management may interface very closely with project managers through project initiating and planning stages but should remain at a distance during execution stages unless needed for priority setting and conflict resolution.[25] However, top management may descend on the project if they feel they are not getting accurate information regarding the status of the project or evident problems at *any* stage. To avoid such difficulties, project managers must provide meaningful status reports on a regular basis.

Project managers must recognize top management's role, management style, and philosophies. They must develop skills to work with top management effectively and try to win their support and confidence for successful management of the project.

Functional/line managers

Functional or line managers play a vital role in the project environment. They may represent various departments or technical areas that share responsibilities in order to meet project objectives. Functional/line managers are responsible for the primary functions of the organization such as marketing, production, engineering, etc. The main elements of the role of a functional manager are:[25]

- *How* the task will be done (define technical criteria)
- *Where* the task will be done (define facilities required if there is a choice)
- *Who* will do the job (provide alternate resources based on competency and availability).

Functional managers may act like line managers for some work packages after the project manager has identified what work has to be done and the constraints associated with it. Normally for large projects, resources (human and others) are identified (in terms of their competency and availability) and requested by the project manager, but are assigned and controlled by functional managers. In a fully projectized environment, functional managers and their group members work full-time for the project manager. This is a simpler, more hierarchical structure but may be expensive for the organization if these resources are not fully utilized.

However, in projects organized as a matrix, project management does not follow the principle of "unity of command." Rather, it is based upon shared authority and responsibility between the project managers and functional managers. In such an environment, functional/line managers are under a lot of pressure to fulfill their commitments to the project managers. Project managers plan, monitor and control the project whereas the functional managers are responsible for performing the work. In some instances, the functional manager may face conflicts of interest in allocating the best resources for his or her own departmental project, which may not be effective for organization as a whole. This problem can be partially resolved if top manage-

Figure 2.5 Project Functional Interface

Project Manager	Functional Manager
• *What* is to be done?	• *How* will the task be done?
• *When* will the task be done?	• *Where* will the task be done?
• *Why* will the task be done?	• *Who* will do the task?
• *How* much time and money is available to do the task?	• *How well* has the functional input been integrated into the project?
• *How well* has the total project been done?	

ment evaluates functional managers on the basis of how well they are cooperating with project managers and living up to their commitments.[25]

In an organization with several active projects, functional or line managers may have to cope with:[25]
- Unlimited work requests (especially during competitive bidding)
- Limited availability of resources
- Predetermined and unrealistic deadlines
- All requests having a high priority
- Unscheduled changes in the project plan
- Unpredicted lack of progress
- Unplanned breakdown of resources
- Labor strikes and work stoppages
- Unplanned loss of resources due to turnover, illness, and absenteeism.

Practically, project managers must have some reasonable contingencies to cope with uncertainties. The project manager should not and cannot expect to have the best resources all the time. Functional managers should not commit to an availability of specific people for any project but rather make a commitment in meeting the project requirements within scope, quality, time, and cost constraints. The project manager should track and monitor that portion of the project and demand better resources only if and when the project manager can convince the functional manager that the resources assigned are not appropriate.[26] Project managers should do this by using their negotiating and interpersonal skills carefully, delicately, and diplomatically to avoid undesirable confrontation. Interfacing factors between the project manager and functional manager are shown in Figure 2.5.

Functional managers, as permanent, ongoing employees, typically have more organizational authority than members of a project team, which is dissolved at the end of the project. And, although project managers may be able to influence top management because of their successful track records, they are transient figures and as such must rely on their sensitivity and ability to inspire and motivate functional managers to do their best for the project.[20] Top management must encourage a team effort between the project manager and functional manager, because without sincere cooperation and teamwork, projects will fail, and both project managers and functional managers will be the losers.

Staff personnel

Staff personnel work in departments and are accountable for results that affect the process by which line managers accomplish their goals. They are not directly involved in the project's mainstream activity but rather advise, counsel, or provide specialized services to the project.

Staff personnel contribute by providing advice and service to the project manager and line managers in accomplishing organizational goals. They normally give their advice only when requested to do so. However, in a project environment, staff personnel have the moral and ethical responsibility to offer advice and service where it is needed.

It is normally up to line managers to request advice and to accept or reject the suggestions from staff personnel. Staff personnel provide special expertise that may be helpful at different times throughout the life cycle of the project; therefore, line managers should give serious consideration to their observations.

Major roles of staff personnel. Staff personnel play the following three major roles in assisting line managers.[27]

The advisory or counselling role: Staff personnel can be viewed as internal consultants, solving organizational problems by using their professional experience. This relationship between line and staff is similar to that between a professional and a client. For example, in a manufacturing environment, a staff quality control manager can advise the line manager responsible for production about technical modifications to the production process that will enhance the quality of products. Similarly, a finance department can provide financial advice regarding the financing and cash flow implications for projects.

The service role: In this role, centralized staff personnel provide specialized and expert advice that individual projects may not have within their own project group. This can be seen as a relationship between a supplier (staff personnel) and a customer (project managers). For example, for large projects, personnel departments recruit, employ, and train personnel for the whole project and relieve the project manager of this workload. In this way, the personnel department becomes a supplier of workers and the project managers needing those workers are its customers. Similarly, a legal department in an organization may participate actively in

58

preparing contract documents and looking after contract administration, litigation, and other legal activities related to the project, providing legal services in the same way an outside law firm would.

The control role: In this role, experienced staff personnel help establish a mechanism for evaluating the effectiveness of project plans. Staff personnel exercising this role can be viewed as agents of top management and are effective only if they have the respect and confidence of the project managers.

The above three roles are not the only roles performed by staff personnel but they represent the major roles.

Some considerations that should be remembered when using staff personnel are:

- They may form a part of the project team.
- They should be carefully chosen.
- They may come from other departments on temporary assignments for the project or for specific phases in the project life cycle.
- Their role must be clearly defined in terms of responsibility, authority, and accountability.
- They must be given appropriate recognition if and when necessary.

Conflict in line/staff relationships. Most project managers will attest to the existence of noticeable conflict in line-staff relationships.[28] For the life of a project, especially in a fully projectized environment, the project manager fulfills a "line" function. At other times, the project manager plays a "staff" role when requested to give special expert advice or assist in formulating organizational strategies. According to line managers, conflict is created because staff personnel tend to assume line authority, steal credit for success, or fail to give sound advice; they are unable to see the whole picture and do not keep the line managers informed. On the other hand, staff personnel feel that conflict is created because line personnel do not respect and make proper use of staff personnel, resist new ideas, and do not give enough authority to staff personnel.

To overcome these conflicts, staff personnel must emphasize organizational and project objectives, encourage and educate line managers and project managers about how and when to use staff personnel (just as they need to know when and how to use outside consultants), and deal with this universal resistance to change or new ideas through better interpersonal relationships and effective communication. At the same time, line managers should minimize these potential conflicts by using staff personnel whenever possible, incorporating their ideas and suggestions, and keeping staff personnel informed of any special issues, variations, and risks associated with the project.

In a project environment, the role of staff personnel should be carefully identified and designed. It is important that staff personnel always aim to help project managers and line managers do their jobs more effectively and efficiently. To be cost effective, they must earn the trust, respect, and confidence of project managers and functional/line managers and increase their acceptance of advice and recommendations. The project manager must integrate staff personnel into the project team in such a way that they feel themselves to be active participants and contributors.

Service and support personnel

These personnel work in internal operating functions such as personnel, accounting, purchasing, operations, maintenance, etc. They are needed to keep primary project functions operating effectively. Just as the name suggests, these personnel can make a significant contribution if they view themselves as resources to provide service functions with the primary aim of assisting line managers, project managers, and their teams in meeting project objectives effectively. Project managers should emphasize this "service" attitude as an important element of their organizational culture. Service and support should adopt the attitude that they exist to help the line or project organizations rather than vice versa. They should continually address the question: *What can we do to help the project managers and their team achieve their objectives more effectively and efficiently?*

The major roles and potential conflicts between this group of individuals, project managers, and line managers are conceptually very similar to those of staff personnel, except for the specific roles that service and support personnel play. It helps if detailed plans and procedures associated with their own areas are developed to suit the overall project plan.

Sometimes it is better to make this group of individuals a part of the project team because they perform primary functions in the project. Since they may not be required on a full-time basis, one person from these service and support departments may support more than one project at a time. In addition to their normal service and support functions, individuals from purchasing, accounting, and finance may also play different roles depending on the type, size, and complexity of the project. Priority conflicts should be resolved through effective communication and interpersonal skills, emphasizing the importance of considering the welfare of the organization as a whole.

Because the project manager depends upon continuous cooperation from service and support personnel, he or she must encourage a supportive role and relationship, providing appropriate evaluation and training to help them perform project functions effectively. The project manager should encourage their sincere and active participation throughout the life cycle of the project through effective communication. It is important that they get the feeling of "ownership" of the project plan and see themselves as an integral and important part of the project organization.

Other project managers

In organizations with several ongoing projects, project managers must also interact with other project managers, who may or may not have similar backgrounds, norms, and cultures. In many cases, it is helpful if some kind of formal or informal system is established within the organization to encourage open communications between them. Some of the major types of exchanges and interactions among project managers are:

General information exchange. A general information exchange is especially useful if projects are diverse. In some organizations, a formal "project information exchange group" meets once or twice a month to exchange information and experiences. This can help the organization train project staff in the various areas in which the organization is involved.

Exchange of information on project management tools and techniques. Project managers can talk about various methodologies, tools, and practices used in their projects. New ideas emerge and old ones are reinforced as a result of such interaction. Hardware and software problems can be defined and resolved by exchanging ideas and experiences.

Exchange of information on human resources. This type of information exchange helps project managers find specialists that could be critical to their project and that might be available on a short-term basis from other projects. Project managers can stand in for each other and discuss the strengths and weaknesses of key human resources. Overall personnel constraints can be defined and their impact on various projects can be evaluated, optimizing personnel allocation. It should be noted that all project managers may not share information about human resources fully, freely, or in good faith—for example, they may be willing to transfer the personnel they are trying to get rid of.

Exchange of information on skills. Project managers can discuss their experiences related to technical, human, and interpersonal skills. This helps them learn from each other and increase their self-confidence in dealing with project management problems and issues. Such exchanges are useful when project managers are involved in multinational projects characterized by cultural diversity, requiring them to be knowledgeable about cultural differences and their influence on project success. This concept of exchanging skills with others will help train project managers involved in different industries, countries, and environments.

Because of tough global competition, there is an increasing trend towards "management by projects" to manage the whole organization. The survival and growth of these "projectized" organizations will depend upon the quality of their project managers, and upon their ability to interact and cooperate with each other. Open and continuous communication is the key to realizing maximum gain by sharing experiences with other project managers. Top management should not only encourage, but should make these interactions an important element of the organizational operating climate.

THE INTERNAL ENVIRONMENT OF THE PROJECT is one of the most vital elements of project structure. Project managers may rotate from project to project and have different clients and external stakeholders, but they generally have to deal with the same members of their home organizations.

Therefore, they must spend some energy in influencing the project's internal operating environment for the benefit of all internal stakeholders. The attitudes of *we care* and *teamwork* must be developed and practiced. Internal stakeholders must be viewed as an integral part of the team responsible for meeting project objectives.

By encouraging the active participation of all internal stakeholders from the beginning and throughout the life cycle of the project, project managers gain their acceptance and hence their commitment to implementing plans effectively. Every decision and action should be designed to enrich these stakeholders' experiences. The project management approach should focus more on the quality of stakeholders' experience at every stage of the project than on an overriding preoccupation with computer printouts and weekly progress reports.

Internal stakeholders should refrain from blaming each other for failure and emphasize helping each other to win. Senior managers should discourage negative attitudes at the outset of the project, creating a conducive environment that facilitates *true* teamwork among all internal stakeholders. They should encourage and support project managers, line/functional managers, and service and staff personnel. Effective communication and interpersonal skills are essential to coordinate and integrate the efforts of all internal stakeholders.

Interfacing with Contractors and Subcontractors

Open communication and fair working relationships enhance trust and mutual benefits.

Contractors and subcontractors have been placed into a separate category because they may be classified as internal or external stakeholders depending upon the circumstances. For example, sometimes external consultants with special expertise and knowledge may be hired to augment the project team. They may be given full responsibility and authority to carry out some specific technical activities (e.g., procurement and installation of computer systems, inspection and testing of technical equipment) or project management assignments (e.g., cost estimates, schedule, setting up quality control procedures). Although they are not permanent employees of the organization, they become members of the project team for as long as needed and participate actively in decision making and the overall project management process. In such circumstances, they are project participants and can be classified as internal stakeholders because they are directly associated with the project outcome and provide inputs as required to obtain the project objectives.

On the other hand, contractors and subcontractors may be considered external stakeholders when they are brought in to perform a specific task. In such circumstances, the interest of contractors is limited to meeting their own contractual obligations. They are primarily concerned about their own

Organizing Projects for Success

organization's priorities and welfare and may not be committed to long-term or overall success of the project, as are the internal stakeholders. However, contractors and subcontractors are still generally concerned about project success. Maintaining good relationships with the project manager and the key project team members increases their chances of repeat business.

Even with internal projects, project managers are often involved in one or more contracts, so project success depends a great deal on understanding techniques for negotiating and administering contracts with contractors and subcontractors. It is also important to identify risks and understand techniques of allocating and managing risks. The project manager then assumes the role of a contract manager, ensuring that contractors and subcontractors meet their obligations regarding scope, quality, time, and cost constraints. Though project managers do not have to be lawyers, they must recognize the legal aspects of project activities and be aware of their implications, obtaining legal assistance when necessary.

In order to limit liability and share risks, project managers must be aware of the various types of clauses to be negotiated when finalizing a contract. They must also be aware of effective ways to administer contracts in order to avoid disputes and litigation.

Contract clauses

Contracts are both a critical source of liability exposure as well as a source of protection. Project managers must be able to identify potential liability exposure and construct clauses to limit this exposure consistent with responsibility. Cleland has outlined some of the clauses that must be carefully defined, understood and implemented in order to limit liability.[29]

Contract administration

Project managers must possess good contract administration skills, one of the most important components of contract management. This includes supervising the work to be done under the terms of the contract, preparing and processing change orders, providing interpretation of contract language, and approving invoices as the work is completed. Project managers must realize that any shortcoming in fulfilling these responsibilities could lead to charges of negligence either against the project manager, project team members, or the parent organization. Recommendations for administering contracts in managing projects include:[29]

- Establish and maintain appropriate control procedures to ensure that the company's most current contracting and compensation policies are being complied with.
- Ensure that all required approvals, signatures, and comments have been secured and documented and that no work is performed without an approved complete contract or a formal *letter of authorization to work*.
- Maintain a contract file that includes all communications regarding changes in scope, work authorization, constraints, and budgets. All

documentation and communication should be on company forms and include the project and/or job number.

- Design and implement a proper system to deal with change orders because this may substantially change the total cost of the project. Clear documentation of all changes, the price changes involved, and authorization to proceed must be kept in contract files. This is most critical to the successful completion of the contract and, if not well-managed, is a potential area for litigation.

Successful management of contractors and subcontractors includes understanding risk allocation and being able to implement risk allocation concepts when negotiating and administering contracts. Project managers must be able to construct contract clauses that minimize the liability exposure of their organizations. They must understand the value of formal legal assistance in finalizing contracts, avoiding costly and lengthy legal settlements that are disruptive to themselves, their employers, and project teams. Major contractors should be invited to participate in the conceptual and developmental phase of the project life cycle and encouraged to make any suggestions during these early stages in order to avoid costly changes at a later date.

Interfacing with External Stakeholders and the Environment

The world steps aside to let pass the people who know where they are going.
— Anonymous

Project managers must coordinate internal actions with the external environment, which has significant influence on project success. The external environment may vary according to the type, size, and nature of the project. For large projects, in-depth analysis of the external environment may be necessary because of the amount at stake. The project's external environment includes aspects such as:

- Its technology (associated advances, opportunities, and constraints)
- The nature of its products
- Customers and competitors
- Its geographical setting
- Its social and political environment
- Its environmental and legal impacts
- Its economic, employment and technological impacts.

Most of the uncertainty in projects comes from factors in the external environment. One technique helpful in managing the external environment of the project is to prioritize the various stakeholder linkages, i.e., relationships among various stakeholders, by conducting a stakeholder analysis. However, the extent and mix of linkages will vary from project to project. These linkages can be analyzed to define potential problems, to assess the probability of their occurrence, and to try to solve them ahead of time. This analysis involves identifying all the potential external stakeholders and determining their relative ability to influence the project outcome.[4]

64

When dealing with external stakeholders, it is important to distinguish between the "product of the project" versus the "project itself." Sometimes, projects may encounter significant problems because of public concerns about and perceptions of the impact of the project on their community. For example, a concern about building a highway in a specific location is related to the "product of the project," while concern about dust and traffic delays during construction are a concern with the project itself. *PM Network* has published several interesting stories describing the challenges in interfacing with external stakeholders who have a direct and/or indirect influence on the project management process and its final product. These challenges involve listening to external stakeholders and then understanding and resolving the major issues which include concerns about the physical appearance of the project product or facilities; impacts on neighborhoods and communities; general public concerns; social and cultural concerns; regulatory concerns; environmental and legal problems; and economic concerns.[30]

For large, complex projects, analysis of the external environment becomes very challenging and may need special technical and human skills and knowledge acquired from outside. Especially for international projects, project managers must have some knowledge, understanding, and appreciation of different cultural backgrounds, social and political systems, and even languages in order to negotiate project issues with international partners.

External factors, and particularly changes in them, can significantly affect the project management process and hence project success.[31] Some of the main categories of external stakeholders or third parties who may require special attention during the project life cycle are shown in Figure 2.6.

Regulatory concerns

The task of individuals who work for government and/or regulatory agencies is to ensure compliance with their particular agency's requirements. For example, they may:

- Oversee the project, ensuring that it stays within the regulations and bylaws set by national, regional and local governments
- Act as liaison between such governments and the project manager
- Clarify the regulations whenever necessary
- Assist a project manager in reviewing the long-term and short-term effects of regulations and the effect of any anticipated changes in regulations on specific projects.

These people should not be viewed merely as watchdogs. They can be quite helpful in meeting project objectives through effective communication and interpersonal skills. Although ensuring that the project meets the standards set forth, regulatory personnel can also monitor and point out when the project fails to meet these standards. Such occurrences, if caught at the early stages, can help reduce the project's costs and duration.

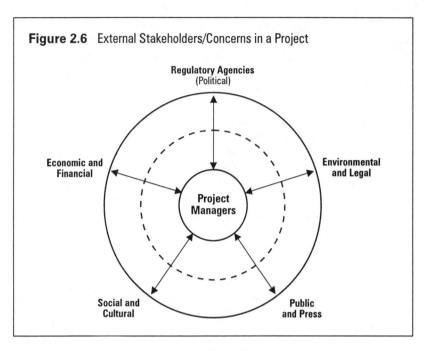

Figure 2.6 External Stakeholders/Concerns in a Project

Regulatory Agencies
(Political)

Economic and
Financial

Environmental
and Legal

Project
Managers

Social and
Cultural

Public
and Press

Because of the nature of the work, and because regulators are responsible and accountable to the public at large, they usually have certain discretionary powers, i.e., the ability to shut down job sites or to recommend fines or penalties for violating certain laws and regulations. Project managers should try to involve the regulators in the relevant parts of the project plan right from the start in order to gain their acceptance. Their increased commitment to help meet project objectives will minimize any potential adverse effects on the project.

Quite often, projects related to the nuclear industry have experienced significant problems because regulations are being defined and developed while the facilities are already under construction. This results in revising designs, changing major equipment, and altering construction techniques.

Environmental and legal concerns
Environmental and legal concerns play important roles in our lives. Since the environment affects the quality of life, it is associated with labor, political, social, technological and economic issues. Environmentally concerned individuals align themselves with the various groups concerned with issues of protecting the environment. For example, large chemical and petrochemical plants may emit pollutants which, if not treated or checked, will adversely affect the environment, leading to health and water contamination problems. The main job of environmentally concerned personnel is assessing environmental impacts before, during and after a

66

project is undertaken. Monitoring the impact on the environment helps define realistic goals for the project and the organization as a whole.

Project managers should work with this group of representatives as a team in order to expedite the project and obtain necessary clearances from environmental protection agencies. The regulatory processes should be used as elements of good planning, rather than being viewed as obstacles to the accomplishment of project objectives. For example, the Atigun Mainline Reroute Project in Alaska experienced interesting environmental constraints that were resolved by incorporating them into the overall plans and managing them accordingly.[32]

Legal concerns include ensuring that the project complies with all aspects of the law, especially as new laws are passed and old ones are eliminated. Attention to legal concerns provides opportunities to limit risk to organizations and increase benefits in the short- and long-term. Legal advisors generally make sure that anything done by the project manager and the project team will have limited repercussions and that all necessary permits, licenses, etc., are in good order. These personnel are looking out for the good of the project, company, and project clients, so the project manager must keep them informed of all aspects of the project—especially problems and issues that may have legal implications. The project manager must also recognize the legal impacts of project management techniques and practices and should get expert legal help when and if necessary.

The public and the press

For high-profile projects, public relations is an important component which influences the general external environment. The public includes all those who are not directly involved in the project but who have an interest in its outcome. This could include, for example, environmental protection groups, equal opportunity groups, the local community, and others with a real or imagined interest in the project or the way it is managed. The project managers must try to sell the project to the public by emphasizing the benefits and positive impacts of the project. The intangible and long-term nature of these benefits should be emphasized to justify the project. Community leaders may influence the project outcome and therefore they should be invited to participate in formulating preliminary project plans and in strategies to "sell" the project to the general public. The project manager must either play the role of spokesperson for the project or delegate this vital function to a capable person on the team. Some of the main points about which project managers may be obliged to inform the public and press are:

- General impact of the project (e.g. environmental safety, socio–economic, overall urban planning, transportation, etc.)
- Project's compliance with the letter and the intent or spirit of the law and compatibility with relevant regulations and bylaws

- Project's contribution to overall growth of the community
- Technological, economic, and employment spin-offs in the short-term and long-term
- Project's role at an international level. For example, some large scientific projects may play a leadership role in technological spin-offs or in a specific area of unique research, which should be emphasized to justify funding.

Good public relations is an essential part of successful project management. A well-planned and organized PR program helps manage the stakeholders by maintaining adequate project communications that promote good understanding of the project; by keeping the "public" (internal and external) up-to-date on the progress and performance of the project; and by responding to any misleading information about the project.[33]

Developing a good PR program for the project requires establishing a variety of contacts. The contacts for a typical PR program include:[33]

- Project workforce and project users
- Professional, business and labor groups
- Local community and the community at large
- Elected representatives and government administrators
- News media and the business media
- Educators and school groups
- Taxpayers
- Industrial sector of the project and special interest groups.

Thus, project managers must be aware of the socially, culturally, and environmentally sensitive issues associated with their projects. They must appreciate the importance of the roles that the public and press can play in making or breaking their projects. For example, project managers of the Westlake Project worked with the community and resolved the problems of business owners who were likely to be affected by the project itself and its management process.[34]

Project managers should evaluate potential impacts of the project on the community and address major concerns of the public. For example, at Boeing's modern spare parts distribution facility located near a residential community adjacent to the Seatac airport, community concerns about the new facility included the appearance of the facility and its impact on the community. To resolve this, the building was lowered approximately 20 feet in the southeast corner, indirect lighting was used to prevent perimeter and parking lot lighting from projecting into the neighborhood, and the landscaping of an area adjacent to the neighborhood with a meandering path and signs identifying the plantings. Project managers also recognized that it was important to make friends of the neighbors by being sensitive to their concerns, and keeping them well informed during the construction process.[35]

Organizing Projects for Success

Stakeholders have a major impact on the success of projects. Sometimes these groups or individuals appear in most unexpected manners and at most inopportune times. Society requires that they be dealt with, one way or another. Milwaukee Water Pollution Abatement Program documents the case for being proactive in this regard.[36] The project manager used effective communication and considered all the stakeholders. The project management team was convinced that public relations and law firms, which understand the social and political complexities as well as the engineering basics of a project, are essential members of project teams. They recognized that the costs of ignoring any stakeholder are too high.

Because they introduce environmental and social concerns that delay the schedule and increase total costs, the public and press carry a negative image and are perceived as potential threats to completing projects on time and within budget. However, to be successful, project managers must plan for these problems and communicate effectively with the public and the press to overcome such obstacles.

Social and cultural concerns

Social, cultural, and economic concerns are highly interrelated. Some projects may have strong social and cultural aspects that may affect the economic situation of the project and its stakeholders. Project managers should appreciate and understand the impacts of demographics and social values (associated with work ethics) of project participants in order to staff and organize projects effectively.

Social concerns. An important aspect of the general environment, the social component describes characteristics of the society and the social environment in which the project operates. Two important features of society are commonly studied during environmental analysis.[37]

Demographics are the statistical characteristics of the population, including changes in the number of people and their income distribution. These changes can influence the types and nature of projects and recruitment strategies, depending upon the availability and corresponding cost of human resources, especially technical specialists.

Social values refer to the relative degree of importance that society places on the ways in which it exists or functions. Social values can change dramatically over a period of time, influencing the organizational environment and hence project performance. For example, the general work ethic of project participants towards work, openness to training or learning new techniques, professional opportunities, rewards and expectations, motivational and communication strategies, etc., can seriously affect project success. The project manager should realize that differences in social values are inevitable and try to create a project environment compatible with the social values of the project participants.[38]

Social and cultural concerns can have a significant impact on the project management process. The success story of the rebirth of the New Orleans riverfront illustrates how project managers resolved social concerns of the public who were likely to be affected by the project.[39] It is an excellent example of true partnership in urban development where developers, business owners, local governments, and the public at large worked as a real team.

Cultural concerns. The culture surrounding a project (both internal and external) has a significant impact on its ultimate success. This culture includes the organizational culture, work climate, and the culture of the various project participants. The issues of cultural diversity and how they affect the project management process should not be overlooked. Organizational climate and culture depends upon:

- General philosophy and managerial style of top management (e.g., autocratic, participative, etc.)
- Organizational structure of the project (vertical, horizontal, functional, free form, or matrix structure, etc.)
- The nature and maturity level of project participants (low achievers/high achievers, dependent/independent workers, etc.)
- The size and nature of projects (e.g., large, complex, international, level of technological uncertainties, etc.).

Various organizational design options to suit the size, complexity and environment of organizations are discussed in detail in Chapter 5.

The culture of project participants, which includes their values, beliefs, and convictions, strongly influences such important workplace issues as ethics; attitudes toward achievement, training, and supervision; degree of self-motivation; and interpersonal, problem-solving, and conflict resolution skills. Rotation of project managers from project to project should be encouraged. This can help them develop cultural skills and experience that are a definite asset especially on international projects, where a good understanding and appreciation of different cultural values, languages, and special business manners and techniques would be very helpful.

Economic and financial concerns

Economic and financial aspects of a project are important components of the general project environment that must be analyzed and evaluated early in the project's conceptual phase. Some large projects may need an extensive budget for capital and operating costs and may be characterized by varying degrees of business and technological risks. For a large international R&D project, the funding formula might be quite political and complex due to possible contributions from foreign countries. The general economic environment (recession or boom) and various financing alternatives and formulae will determine the overall viability of the project and influence the "go/no go" decision required to commence project implementation. Consequently, the project manager should have a good general understanding and

70

knowledge of project economic and financial aspects.

Project managers should be able to participate in initial analysis and feasibility studies because they have to live with the various options, decisions and constraints. The risk analysis associated with schedule, budget and quality should be done as a part of front-end planning and monitored regularly to determine major deviations and necessary remedial actions. The impact of currency fluctuations and changes in interest rates should be evaluated, especially for international projects. Sometimes this analysis is done in collaboration with customers or client representatives, but in all cases it should have the involvement and support of top management and/or the project sponsor from the home organization.

The external stakeholders are indirectly associated with the project but may have a significant ability to influence the project outcome. These stakeholders are normally outside the authority of the project manager and may present serious project management problems and challenges. Similar to the strategy of influencing internal environment by developing the right attitude of *we care*, *teamwork*, and *participation*, it is important to develop a good relationship and understanding with external stakeholders. They should be involved and kept informed as necessary. A practical strategy is to gain their acceptance to the project plan and make them feel valued members of the team, committed to accomplish project objectives. Their suggestions should be listened to, and proper recognition and credits should be given for their good ideas.

In analyzing the external environment, it should be recognized that external stakeholders may vary throughout the project life cycle. All potential external stakeholders should be identified during each phase of the project and their relative ability to influence determined in order to develop a strategy to manage them. Remember that even a minor stakeholder group may discover a "fatal flaw" in the project plan and slow down the project progress or abort it altogether. Therefore, project managers should keep in constant touch with external stakeholders, continually evaluating their potential impact on the project and encouraging them to work with the project team and contribute towards the project objectives.

Putting it All Together (Stakeholder Analysis)

Stakeholder analysis is the first step in managing project stakeholders. Satisfying the needs and expectations of all project stakeholders is very difficult because they often have different objectives, concerns and constraints. To do the stakeholder analysis, it is important to first identify important items to be used in evaluating project outcome, such as cost schedule, quality/technical performance, and contribution to the organization and/or society. Then, major project stakeholders who will influence the evaluation criteria items must be identified. These may include client/sponsor, project manager, project team, top management, other internal stakeholders, contractors/suppliers and external stakeholders.[40]

Figure 2.7 shows different categories of major project stakeholders and their contributions to evaluation criteria or how they view these criteria. The concept illustrated by Figure 2.7 should be used as a guideline only to analyze the project stakeholders in terms of their primary objectives and concerns. Evaluation criteria and project stakeholders may vary from project to project. Therefore, the project managers should prepare their own analysis tailored to the internal and external environment of the project.

Summary

Projects are like team sports in which all participants play an important role. Effective integration and interface management is the key to successful project management. All projects have different groupings of stakeholders who are affected by the project and interested in its outcome. The project manager must interface effectively with all these stakeholders, earning their trust, cooperation, and confidence and creating an environment where everyone increases each other's effectiveness in meeting project objectives.

Successful management of stakeholders means identifying and analyzing them and recognizing their roles, interests and relationships with other stakeholders. Stakeholders can be classified in two main categories; 1) internal stakeholders who are directly associated with the project and 2) external stakeholders who are indirectly associated with the project. Contractors and subcontractors may play the roles of internal or external stakeholders, depending upon the circumstances and how the project is structured. Meeting needs and expectations of all project stakeholders may be difficult because they often have different objectives and concerns.

Clients or project sponsors, project team members, contractors and subcontractors, and competitors and other special interest groups are also important stakeholders who play a vital role in the project and are very much interested in the project outcome. Project managers must recognize the key features of interfacing with clients/project sponsors, such as areas for client consultation, reporting techniques, the general role of the client regarding enforcement of policies, and procedures. They must acquire appropriate managerial skills, which include effective communication, negotiation and conflict management, in order to satisfy customers.

Internal stakeholders must be viewed as the core elements of the project team, both in perception and in reality. They may include top management, functional managers, staff personnel, service and support personnel, and other project managers. Project managers must develop and practice an attitude of *we care* and *teamwork*. They must encourage active participation of internal stakeholders in order to gain their acceptance, and hence their commitment, in preparing and implementing project

72

Figure 2.7 Stakeholders Analysis for a Sample Project

Stakeholder	Cost	Schedule	Quality/Tech Performance	Contribution to Organization or Society
Client	Meet or beat	Meet or beat	Meet or beat	High
Project Manager	≤ Target	≤ Target	Meets or exceeds specs	High
Contractors/ Subcontractors	Will not mind more money	Wants more time	Meet or beat	NA (want positive visibility)
External	Indifferent	Indifferent	High	Org. – NA Society – High
Project Team	Want flexibility	Want more time to avoid extra pressure	Meet or beat	High
Top Management	Beat	Beat	Meet or beat	High
Other Internal Stakeholders	Want flexibility	Wants more time	Want flexibility	High

Adapted from: Jeffrey K. Pinto. 1994. *Successful Information System Implementation: The Human Side.* Upper Darby, PA: Project Management Institute, p. 124.

plans. Effective communication, negotiation and interpersonal skills are necessary to interface effectively with internal stakeholders.

External stakeholders may be indirectly associated with the project but they may have a significant ability to influence the project outcome. Major concerns of external stakeholders include regulatory concerns, environmental and legal concerns, social, cultural, and economic concerns. The role of public and press should not be overlooked in the project management process.

Project managers must analyze the project's external environment. They must identify all external stakeholders, recognize their roles and ability to influence the project outcome, and then develop an appropriate strategy to gain their support throughout the project life cycle. Project managers must listen to the suggestions of external stakeholders and give them proper recognition for their good ideas, thus encouraging them to minimize the barriers and expedite the project.

*What differentiates companies today is the calibre and
commitment of their staff. Managers recognize this and organize
their human resources effectively as a strategy to manage their
projects*

— *Jim Keyser[1]*

3

Designing Organizational Structures: General Considerations

DESIGNING AN ORGANIZATION is the process of selecting a structure and the formal systems of communication, division of labor, coordination, control, authority, and responsibility necessary to achieve organizational goals. Organizational design requires a decision-making process that takes into account environmental forces, strategic choices, and technological factors. A good organizational design eases the flow of information and decision making, clarifies authority and responsibility, and creates the desired levels of coordination between departments.[2]

According to Lorsch "the design of the organization is composed of the structure, rewards, and measurement practices intended to direct its people's behavior towards the organizational goals."[3] Some general considerations and ingredients for designing organizational structures are:

- The organizing process and how it relates to the planning process
- Classic principles that should be understood and analyzed in order to define chains of command and span of management; balance authority and responsibility; create appropriate division of labor and departmentation
- Dimensions of organizational structure which include formalization, centralization, complexity, and specialization
- Relevant factors associated with the external and internal (operating) environment of the project.

In organizing projects, some modifications may be required to suit the project environment. And aspects of organizational design may vary from project to project depending upon its type of industry, size, complexity, risk factors, technology, and general organizational culture. ∎

About Organizing

There is something that is much more scarce, something rarer than ability. It is the ability to recognize ability.

— Robert Half

In a project environment, the organizing function determines the tasks or activities to be performed, the jobs or positions required to complete the tasks, the resources (human and others) needed to accomplish the task and to meet the project or organizational objectives. Organizing is directly related to and interdependent on planning and therefore should be integrated at the front-end planning phase of the project. Organizing is the process of establishing effective and orderly uses for all resources within the project system and also within the management system as a whole.[2] It emphasizes the attainment of project objectives and helps project managers not only in setting them but also in clarifying which resources will be needed to attain them.

Regardless of the size or nature of the business, every project must have a structure. Organizational structure is the result of the organizing process. Organizational structure is the pattern of formal relationships that exists among project teams and individual team members in an organization. The larger the project, the greater the need for the organizational structure to be properly documented and circulated to everyone primarily involved with the project.

This section deals with the importance of organizing, the organizing process, dimensions of organizational structures and some classic organizing principles that must be understood in order to design a structure which makes it possible to meet project objectives within given constraints of time, budget and technical specifications.

Importance of organizing

Organizing is important because, through this mechanism, project managers implement their plans. Project managers must organize a diverse mix of personnel with differing backgrounds, norms, expectations and areas of expertise into a structure that will meet project needs. Through this process, relationships between project stakeholders are created and maintained by defining:

- Which resources are to be used for specific activities (resource allocation)
- When and where the resources are to be used (resource schedule)
- How the resources will be used (emphasizing planning and directing or leading).

A thorough organizing effort helps the project manager minimize costly weaknesses, such as duplication of effort, idle organizational resources, mismatch between the task and the people, lack of opportunity to learn a variety of skills that may lead to personal growth.

Simply drawing an organizational chart is not enough to ensure successful implementation of a project. In addition to outlining who reports to whom, the overall organizational design should assist project managers in answering "how will the project organization really work?" Hence it must provide for effective interaction among all the project participants.

The organizing process

The organizing process establishes orderly, efficient and effective uses of project resources in order to meet project objectives.[4] Its aim is to expedite communications and to create and maintain relationships between all project resources. This process, which requires an understanding of the skills, knowledge and abilities possessed by team members; the nature of the tasks to be done; the constraints; and the external environment, is critical to achieving an appropriate organizational option. Key stakeholders should participate actively in the organizing process to encourage their acceptance of and commitment to the chosen organizational structure. The outcome should be the best way to organize the overall operation so that project tasks can be performed with minimum conflict.

Seven main steps of the organizing process are:[4,5]

1. *Review project goals and develop conceptual planning.* This is required to define scope and identify major constraints and information requirements.
2. *Establish major tasks required to reach planned goals.* This represents an important link between planning and organizing. Planning sets goals and organizing defines programs, setting out what is to be done, by whom, and with what resources. Tasks that are identified and included in the programs then become the responsibilities of specific organizational units. This step may represent the first level of the work breakdown structure, a "family tree" of project components that organizes and defines the total scope of the project.[5]
3. *Subdivide major tasks into sub-tasks or activities.* Tasks can be further broken down using a work breakdown structure and then assigned in part or in total to people with appropriate skills and knowledge. This up-division creates the working level of the work breakdown structure which, in some industries, may be referred to as "work packages."
4. *Assign specific responsibilities to individuals.* After identifying the skills and knowledge needed to execute specific tasks, individuals are assigned responsibilities to match their skills. Where existing personnel cannot handle the project responsibilities adequately, training new people and/or obtaining outside assistance may be necessary to meet project requirements.
5. *Provide the necessary resources.* In order for individuals to accomplish their assigned tasks, the project manager must ensure that they are given an appropriate level of authority, responsibility and training, along with adequate time, money, materials, personnel and/or information.
6. *Design the appropriate organizational relationships.* Involves designing an organizational hierarchy to facilitate the execution of tasks by

providing a proper arrangement of authority and responsibility to oversee the execution and completion of assignments. The principles of organizing and the overall organizational climate should be considered when designing a hierarchy that may be completely new or modify an existing one.

7. *Evaluate results of organizational strategy.* Involves gathering feedback on how well the implemented strategy is working and collecting information that can be used to improve the existing organization.

In a typical project, Steps 1 to 3 constitute planning, Steps 5 to 7 constitute organizing, and Step 4 serves as an interface and links planning and organizing in the project management process. This very important step requires effective communication and negotiation skills by the project manager. The project manager must work with the functional managers, getting their full commitment by encouraging their active participation in and acceptance of the planning steps (Steps 1 to 3). The interface between planning and organizing can be facilitated with proper support and endorsement from top management.

These steps take place within both the internal and external project environment. This seven-step organizing process should be repeated in each phase of the project life cycle to make potential improvements based on feedback from the previous phase.

Another way of looking at this process is to condense the seven steps into four that organize projects by developing the work breakdown structure and assigning the work packages to appropriate people with matching skills. In some industries, this is known as an *organizational breakdown structure.* The four-step process is as follows:

1. Determine what is to be done (review project goals and develop conceptual planning; establish major tasks; divide major tasks into sub-tasks).
2. Identify responsibilities (match specific activities to individuals on the basis of skills; provide the necessary resources).
3. Define reporting relationships and authorize performance (design organizational relationships to facilitate and coordinate the project team's efforts).
4. Measure results (evaluate results of the organizing strategy).

The organizing subsystem

Like the planning function, the organizing function can be considered as a subsystem of the overall management system. In a project environment, the primary purpose of the organizing subsystem is to assist in meeting project objectives by providing a rational and efficient approach to using organizational resources. Figure 3.1 shows the main ingredients of the organizing subsystem.[4] The input to a specific project is composed of a portion of the total resources of the organization. The process is the seven-step organizing process discussed earlier, and the output is an organizational structure for

Figure 3.1 A Typical Organizing Subsystem

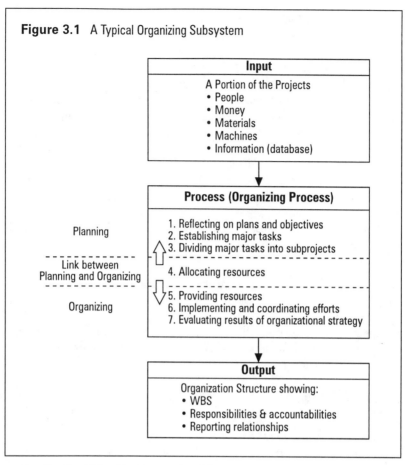

| **Input** |
| A Portion of the Projects |
| • People |
| • Money |
| • Materials |
| • Machines |
| • Information (database) |

| **Process (Organizing Process)** |
| 1. Reflecting on plans and objectives |
| 2. Establishing major tasks |
| 3. Dividing major tasks into subprojects |
| 4. Allocating resources |
| 5. Providing resources |
| 6. Implementing and coordinating efforts |
| 7. Evaluating results of organizational strategy |

Planning

Link between
Planning and Organizing

Organizing

| **Output** |
| Organization Structure showing: |
| • WBS |
| • Responsibilities & accountabilities |
| • Reporting relationships |

Adapted from: Samuel C. Certo. 1994. Modern Management: Diversity, Quality, Ethics, and the Global Environment, Sixth Edition. Englewood, NJ: Prentice-Hall, p. 215. Reprinted by permission of Prentice-Hall, Upper Saddle River, NJ.

the project. For complex projects, it may be appropriate to repeat the organizing process (but at an appropriate level of detail) as the project progresses from phase to phase of the project life cycle. Also, each phase could be considered as a project in its own right and managed accordingly. The project organization should clearly show the major tasks to be done, allocation of responsibility and accountability to carry out the tasks, and key relationships among internal and external project participants in order to enhance communication and implementation.

Organizing is one of the key functions of a project manager, requiring a combination of analytical and human skills. Project managers must understand the importance of organizing, the organizing process, and the organizing subsystem.

Classic Organizational Principles

If there is a way to do it better, find it.

— *Thomas A. Edison*

To set the stage for a discussion of project organization, it is first necessary to review the classic organizational principles used in traditional management. A number of traditional organizing principles have been developed by research scholars and management practitioners. These principles can help project managers avoid falling victim to the most common pitfalls of organizing. However, it should be recognized that there are also exceptions to these principles. Therefore, they should be used as guidelines only and should be applied with flexibility according to the situation. Sometimes it may be necessary to modify these classical principles to suit the project environment.

Some of the most widely known principles applicable to organizing a project or a program are listed below.[6]

Unity of command

This principle requires each element of an organization to be under one boss. No one in the project organization should have more than one boss to whom he or she is accountable. This helps prevent conflicting orders and instructions. However, this principle is purposely violated in a matrix environment (to be discussed later), which is typical for large projects where project team members get directions from project managers *and* their home base functional managers. This principle is often violated when an individual attempts to meet the conflicting requirements of various staff functions in addition to those of a direct supervisor for project tasks.

Parity in authority and responsibility

The main theme of this principle is that a person responsible for doing a certain task must be given sufficient authority to do it or to get it done by others. This is an important principle for project managers or task managers wishing to delegate responsibilities to other project participants in order to be able to concentrate their own efforts. Proper delegation enables managers to advance and also provides training and growth opportunities for the individuals to whom the tasks are delegated. However, many project organizations create situations where responsibility is not commensurate with authority.

Scaler principle (chain of command)

According to this principle, which is related to unity of command, a clear, unbroken line of authority should run from the top to the bottom of an organization. It implies that all members in the organization will communicate with each other by "going through the proper channels," i.e., following the chain of command.

80

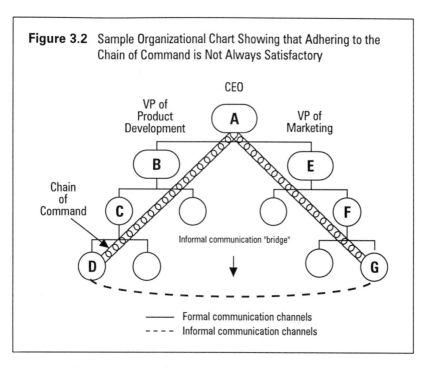

Figure 3.2 Sample Organizational Chart Showing that Adhering to the Chain of Command is Not Always Satisfactory

Strict adherence to the chain of command for communication or getting information in an organization leads to unnecessary bureaucracy and is not advisable. This rationale is illustrated in Figure 3.2, which shows that if individual D (from New Product Development) needs some information from individual G (working under a different manager in Marketing), he or she is expected to go through C, B, A, E, and F. Then, G must reply through F, E, A, B, and C. Obviously this long, involved process is not only slow and expensive but also creates more links where communication may break down. The concept is well illustrated by playing the old party game of transmitting a message sequentially around a circle of individuals. The final message received by the last person is usually significantly distorted compared to the original message. This is because of the many links involved and a tendency to lose meaning and/or introduce some distortion in the message at each link.

In a project environment, such communication problems can be resolved by using a bridge that allows D to go directly to G for information (shown by the dotted line in Figure 3.2). Such bridges are particularly useful for programs/projects dealing with development of new products as they facilitate concurrent engineering. However, such bridges should be used with care and diplomacy so that the managers (A, B, C, E, and F) do not react negatively or feel bypassed. This can be achieved either by getting pre-approval of these managers or by keeping them informed.[4,7]

Designing Organizational Structures: General Considerations

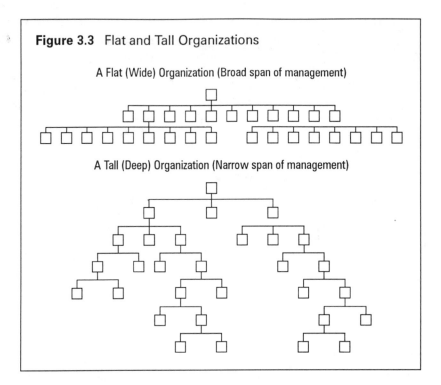

Figure 3.3 Flat and Tall Organizations

A Flat (Wide) Organization (Broad span of management)

A Tall (Deep) Organization (Narrow span of management)

The span of management

Span of management refers to the number of subordinates that report directly to a manager. The fewer individuals a manager supervises, the smaller (narrower) the span of management, while managers with a relatively large number of subordinates reporting to them have the greater (wider) span of management. Span of management is also called span of control, span of authority, span of supervision, and span of responsibility.

A definite relationship exists between span of management and the shape of an organization. In the organization chart, chain is vertical and span is horizontal. As shown in Figure 3.3 a broad span of management indicates a flat (wide) organization chart, while a narrow span indicates a tall (deep) organization chart. A large organization might well be both wide and deep. It is generally recognized that in a project environment, the optimum number of positions reporting to one supervisor should not exceed six or seven.

A narrow span of management allows closer supervision of employees. However, it may not be effective because it creates more levels of hierarchy and because communication may be filtered at each level. Also, when managers are able to supervise more people, especially if the subordinates are mature, independent, and self-motivated individuals, their supervisory potential may not be fully used. On the other hand, a wide span of management allows greater freedom to employees because managers cannot

82

Figure 3.4 Factors Affecting Span of Control and Project
Organizations

Factors	Effect	Guideline
1. The technical competence of the project manager and project team members	1. The greater the competence, the wider the span of control may be	1. Competent teams may be given more autonomy (Self-Directed Project Teams)
2. Desirable degree of interaction among project team members	2. The greater the required interaction, the narrower the span should be	2. Clear, frequent and fast information exchange (use information technology)
3. Administrative workload on the project manager	3. The greater the amount of administrative work, the narrower the span should be	3. Hire a project administrator to offload the project manager
4. The similarity of project tasks and activities	4. The greater the similarity of tasks and activities, the greater the span may be	4. Less number of teams covering more functions
5. Standardized procedures and policies	5. The greater the standardization, the greater the span may be	5. Fewer ad hoc controls and authorizations needed
6. The physical proximity of the project team	6. The closer the proximity, the greater the span may be	6. Organize as a tighter matrix, with most team members in one physical location.
7. Maturity level of the project team	7. Mature project teams can take on increased responsibilities	7. Empower project teams and organize in a flexible and free structure

Adapted from: Frederick A. Starke and Robert W. Sexty. 1992. Contemporary Management in Canada Scarborough, Ont: Prentice Hall Canada Inc., p. 217. Reprinted by permission of the publisher.

provide close supervision. Sometimes it may be better because it prevents micro-management, whereas in other cases it may not allow managers sufficient time needed to resolve some critical aspects of the project. It may also force the managers to delegate more authority to subordinates, which both of them may or may not be able to handle.

Early research on the span of management tried to determine the ideal span of management, i.e., how many individuals a manager can effectively supervise.[8] Failure to find an ideal span of control or management emphasized the importance of identifying those factors that influence the number of subordinates a manager can effectively supervise.[9] Several factors must be analyzed before deciding on an ideal span of control, as shown in Figure 3.4.[10]

Flexibility

Designing flexibility into project organizations increases their capability to react to changing conditions as the project progresses. Project managers must periodically review the organization's resilience and adaptability to new situations and must balance "what is" with "what should have been." Attention should be given to the subtle changes proposed and implemented by project team members themselves because very often they incorporate changes that increase overall effectiveness and efficiency in managing the project.

Division of labor

Division of labor is a consideration in organizing project efforts and is decided after developing the work breakdown structure for the project. The division of labor refers to assigning various portions of a particular task among a number of project team members or other project participants. Rather than one individual doing the entire job, several individuals perform different parts of the total task. In essence, individuals specialize in doing part of the task rather than the entire task. This is very typical in a manufacturing industry (such as an automobile production line, electronic products with numerous components, aircraft manufacturing). Several explanations have been offered for using this principle as an organizing strategy.

Advantages and disadvantages of division of labor. Division of labor may be efficient and have economic benefits. Some of its main advantages are:[4]

- Increases skill in performing a particular task (due to specialization)
- Increases efficiency (less time lost when moving from one task to another)
- Increases sense of ownership (workers design ways to increase their efficiency and solve problems)
- Increases understanding of the job (repetition and practice makes them perfect).

In spite of these advantages, there are limits to the use of extreme division of labor or specialization.[11] Counterarguments stress that the division of labor focuses solely on efficiency and economic benefits (which may be short-term only) and overlook the human aspects. Generally, extremely specialized work becomes boring after some time and therefore results in reduced productivity and quality. Clearly some balance is needed between specialization and human aspects to motivate project team members on an ongoing basis.

Division of labor and coordination. The importance of effective coordination becomes obvious when different individuals are doing related portions of a work. Coordination can be defined as the orderly arrangement of group effort to provide unity of action in the pursuit of a common purpose.[12] Coordination encourages completion of individual portions of a task in a synchronized order that is appropriate for the overall product. Network diagrams prepared during the planning phase showing the sequence of activities should help achieve this coordination.

Departmentation

Departmentation is only applicable to large, complex and geographically dispersed projects. It means grouping functions or major work activities into semi-autonomous units. Similar or related functions in a project cre-

84

ate similar problems and require individuals with similar levels of knowledge, experience and training to deal with them.

This is one of the common methods of establishing formal relationships between resources on a large project. Basically, a department is a group of resources established by the project leaders to perform some specific organizational task. The process of establishing departments is called "departmentation" or "departmentalization." Two questions that must be answered when considering departmentation are:[6]

1. What functions are similar enough to be grouped together?
2. What basis should be used for departmentation?

Grouping similar functions. Ideally, the work in each department is unique. The manager of such a department then knows exactly the activities of each worker. However, in practice, this is not possible in project work and therefore the organization has to group the jobs that are merely similar. Even with this approach, there are several factors that complicate matters when grouping the functions.[6]

Volume of work. Dissimilar functions are sometimes grouped together for organizational convenience when there is not sufficient volume of work to allow specialization.

Formal work rules or traditions. Tasks may be similar but trade practices may prevent them from being assigned to one department. For example, though installing electrical conduits, gas lines, and water pipes are similar, electricians install electrical conduits, gas fitters install gas lines and plumbers install water pipes because of trade restrictions, different regulations, codes, and safety standards.

Functional duplication across several departments. Some functions may be needed for more than one department. For example, inventory control is associated with both purchasing and production departments but it is not clear in which department to place this function.

Conflict of interest. Grouping functions may create a conflict of interest. For example, the quality control function is important to production, but to ensure that objective decisions are made about quality, the quality control inspectors should not be responsible to the production manager.

Need for coordination. Dissimilar functions may have to be combined to coordinate activities. For example, buying/selling for a small computer equipment store or scheduling and cost estimating for a small project are so interdependent that one person may be responsible for both. When the organization becomes larger, different personnel may be needed to manage these functions but their roles and activities must be coordinated to optimize organizational success.

Bases of departmentation. Once the issue of grouping similar functions is settled, the management must decide whether or not the project should be divided into several departments. It is essential to identify the overall organizational strategy and decide on the criterion to be used to form departments. The most widely used bases of departmentation are:[4,6]

Departmentation by function. This is the most traditional and probably the most common way to group functions. Units or departments are formed on the basis of functions (e.g., R&D, engineering, production, marketing) that must be carried out to reach organizational objectives.

Departmentation by product or service. This is used when it is important to focus on the products or services produced. The department is responsible for each product (or group of similar products). It specializes in that product and is fully responsible for the product's success. In other words, the department is a champion of that product. This type of departmentation is used when an organization is providing either a wide range of products or technologically complex products. Product departmentation allows management to give the proper attention to each product. For example, large automobile manufacturers (Ford, General Motors and Chrysler) have several product divisions with broad categories of large and small cars. The departments in some consulting firms may be organized around the services they provide (e.g., design, complete project management services, scheduling/cost estimating services, construction management, R&D, marketing).

Departmentation by customer. Groups of similar customers have similar needs. This is used when an organization wants to focus on satisfying the needs of specific types of customers. For example, a computer equipment firm or a utility might departmentalize on the basis of residential, commercial, educational, and industrial customers. Also, a project management consulting firm may have departments on the basis of clients/customers from different industries, e.g., pulp and paper, utilities, R&D, pharmaceuticals, software development.

Departmentation by territory. Territorial departmentation (e.g., regional, national, international) is used when an organization carries on its activities over large geographic areas. It encourages better service to customers because local personnel know the special needs and problems of their market. For example, some large consulting firms have national and international representatives or offices, which allows them to participate in joint ventures and provide better service for national and international projects. It is becoming increasingly important for most businesses to organize their resources and activities on the basis of work and market locations to compete in a global environment. This makes them more effective in managing the projects characterized by culture diversity and special attributes of international projects.

Departmentation by manufacturing process. This is particularly valid for manufacturing environments. Departments are based upon each major phase of the process used to manufacture the product (assembling, testing, painting, shipping, etc.). This helps management focus on each manufacturing process and how it can be made more effective and efficient.

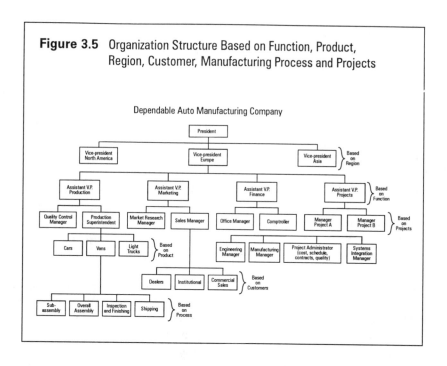

Figure 3.5 Organization Structure Based on Function, Product, Region, Customer, Manufacturing Process and Projects

Dependable Auto Manufacturing Company

Departmentation by project. Program management or project departmentation is typically used when the work of an organization consists of a series of projects with a specific beginning and end. It is often used in the construction industry, defense and aerospace, public sector (utilities, highways), R&D, and high-tech environment (particle accelerator laboratories for basic and applied research, pharmaceutical industries, computers and communication industries), and large industrial projects (pulp and paper, petrochemical, and mining). When a project starts, it is added to the organization chart, and when it is completed, it is taken off the organization chart. Organization charts for firms with many projects are therefore revised frequently.

If a situation warrants, organization charts can be designed by using some or most of the above factors to manage organizational resources effectively. Figure 3.5 integrates the bases of departmentation described earlier to show how all of these factors might be included in the same organization chart for the Dependable Auto Manufacturing Company. Although the classical organizing principles described in this section are generally used in traditional management, they may also be helpful in project management. However, they should be analyzed, evaluated, and implemented carefully to fit the situation, type of the project, project team, project stakeholders, and top management.

Dimensions of Organizational Structure

Organizational structures of projects depend upon their size, complexity and overall organizational climate.

Before designing a project organizational structure, it is important to understand the project's dimensions along with the roles and relationships of participants. The organizational structure of a project can be analyzed along several dimensions.[6]

Formalization

Formalization refers to the degree to which written policies, procedures, rules, and job descriptions guide the behavior of personnel involved in the project. For small projects, the degree of formalization can be quite low and most of the communication and directions are informal, open, and oral. However, for large projects, the degree of formalization is very high, leading to bureaucracy in terms of responsibilities, authority, chains of communication, interpersonal relationships, and decision making. Project managers on large projects use a higher degree of formalization to ensure that activities are done correctly. However, excessive formalization may create "red tape," frustrating project team members and resulting in low morale, low productivity, and low enthusiasm. The mere existence of written rules is no guarantee that the project participants will pay attention to them,[13] but it does help to clarify certain issues and put the project plans in perspective.

Centralization

Centralization deals with how much authority is held at various levels in the organizational hierarchy. In a centralized project environment, the authority to make decisions, especially for operational areas, is highly centralized and the project teams are permitted to initiate actions and make decisions in limited areas only. However, in decentralized projects, authority is dispersed throughout the project organization and the project teams have more freedom in initiating new ideas and making decisions without getting pre-approval of higher management. It must be pointed out that although larger projects are normally more centralized than smaller projects, the degree of centralization may depend upon the maturity level of the participants, the level of confidence of top management in their project teams, and overall philosophy and style of management. Also the degree of centralization may vary according to the project life cycle as the project progresses from the conceptual phase to implementation and termination phases.

Complexity

Complexity covers the number of distinctly different job titles and departments in the project organization. Projects with many different departments and job titles are more complex in terms of integration, interface management, and communication. In such cases, project managers need to have strong human skills in order to manage tasks across several functional boundaries and manage projects effectively with minimum conflicts. They must also formulate and practice an effective communication strategy.

Specialization

Specialization refers to breaking a complex task into simple functional parts so that the individuals or project teams can focus on specific parts of it. For example, project activities could be broken down into conceptual planning, budgeting, estimating, quality control, and information systems development, while engineering design activities could be further broken down into electrical, mechanical, structural, and so on. Functional specialization is widely used in modern organizations for both managerial jobs (legal, marketing, R&D) and operative jobs (production, manufacturing, quality control).

Specialization has advantages and disadvantages. It can be advantageous when it increases efficiency (because the worker refines skills by doing the same small portion of a complex task repetitively). Also, it can allow a manager to supervise large numbers of workers who do an identical task. Specialized jobs can be learned faster because of the limited variety of job skills required. And, in complex projects or organizations, input from specialized units can be vital.

However, a high degree of specialization often leads to unhappiness and lack of motivation, thus reducing efficiency. The boredom inherent in doing repetitive tasks causes workers to lose interest in their work. Thus, they are less motivated, since they have little opportunity to learn new skills or practice different skills. Also, quality may go down when people become overconfident while performing a task. In terms of the impact on the organization, specialists tend to have a narrow outlook and be unable to see the big picture. Extreme specialization also may cause possessiveness, making workers less able to function in a team environment, or lead to a control mentality in the management hierarchy, restricting creativity and innovation.

PROJECT MANAGERS ARE NORMALLY RESPONSIBLE for motivating, record keeping, coordinating, making work assignments, making personnel decisions, providing technical guidance, setting goals, planning, communicating, leading, training, coaching, and controlling. Yet project managers cannot be best at all of these and the attempt to keep a higher degree of control over all activities only leads to bureaucracy and management hierarchy, inhibiting the creativity of project participants. Good project managers try to design substitutes for unnecessary and ineffective hierarchy so that most of these activities can be delegated to appropriate project team members, which not only challenges them and gives them an opportunity to advance, but may also produce better results. Some of the organizational design features and practices that can be adopted as a substitute for a formal hierarchy are:[14]

Task design. Tasks can be designed so that individuals are responsible for producing the whole production service or report. This reduces the problem of coordination and motivation and encourages more creativity and higher performance.

Information systems. Computers and computer networks encourage self-management, better communication, updating and record keeping which has traditionally been done manually by the project manager.

Reward system practices. Profit-sharing plans and skill-based training and compensation have a positive impact on innovation, coordination and communication.

Financial data. Project managers should give project team members and other key project participants financial data on cost estimates, budgets, profitability and economic performance. When this type of information is available to project participants, it facilitates motivation, coordination, and goal setting.

Supplier/client contact. Control of input (from suppliers and top management) and output (to clients and customers) gives feedback to project teams on how well they are performing and what should be done to improve the results.

Training. Traditional hierarchy can be reduced by encouraging extensive on-the-job peer training, providing skill-based pay, and making project teams more responsible for their own training.

Vision/values. Less hierarchy is needed if people know what to do and why they should do their best. If project leaders and top management provide a clear sense of overall direction, project team members will focus on activities that are consistent with the overall values of the organization.

Emergent leadership. The emergence of informal project team leaders reduces the need for hierarchy.

These substitutes vary depending upon how the organization views hierarchy. Adopting them means moving from a hierarchy-based "command and control" to an empowered approach—one based on *commitment, trust* and *shared responsibility*—to achieve excellence and inspire high team performance.

The above dimensions of organizational structures can significantly impact how the project should be organized. Before designing an organization for a project, it is vital to identify and analyze the important dimensions of formalization, centralization, complexity, and specialization in the parent organization.

Basic Factors in Organizing a Project

The basic questions with regard to any work organization are:
- *What are the critical requirements of the technology? and*
- *What are the characteristics of the human system?*

The challenge lies in matching people and technology.

— *Dr. Hans Van Beinum, Executive Director*
The Ontario Quality of Working Life Centre

The organizational design of a project is critical to its successful management. Environmental forces, strategic choices, and technological factors can influence this design. Some projects require a great deal of specialization (differentiation), integration and interface management depending upon their size, complexity and diversity. This section deals with some of the basic factors and forces that influence the organizational design of a project. The project manager must identify, analyze and evaluate these factors to effectively organize a project.

Organizational design decisions in a project environment (such as centralization/decentralization, or changes in responsibility and authority) may solve one set of problems but create others. Every organizational design has some limitations and the key is to select the organizational design that minimizes their impact.

The three basic factors influencing decisions about the design of a project organization are:[2]
- Environmental forces
- Strategic choices
- Technological factors.

Figure 3.6 shows several variables for each of these factors, as well as organizational design guidelines.[15]

Environmental forces

In assessing environmental forces, project managers and team members should consider:
- The characteristics of the present and future environments, and
- The demands of those environments on the need to process information, cope with uncertainties (marketing, technological, financial), and achieve levels of differentiation (division of labor or specialization) and integration (coordination).

To assess these forces, project managers must identify and analyze the project operating environment, the associated environmental characteristics, and the levels of risk associated with the tasks.

Project operating environment. The task environment of a project influences its organizational design. It includes external stakeholders and forces that directly affect the project.[16] Normally, the functional departments in a large and complex project will specialize in dealing with each major external stakeholder in the task environment.[2] Functional departments establish primary links with external stakeholders. For example:[2]

Designing Organizational Structures: General Considerations

Figure 3.6 Important Factors and Their Effects on Organization Design Decisions

Factors	Simple Variables	Organizational Design Guidelines
Environmental Forces	• Degree of complexity • Degree of dynamism	Analyse the outcomes and acquire skills needed. (Matrix structure may be effective to deal with varying degrees of uncertainty.)
Strategic Choices	• Top management's philosophy • Types of customers • Geographic areas served	Emphasize comfort level of top management to meet customer and operational needs. (Traditional functional with ability to respond to market conditions.)
Technological Factors	• Work-flow uncertainty • Task uncertainty • Task interdependence	Analyze and evaluate uncertainty in task and work flow. (Task force or matrix structure may be effective.)

Adapted from: Don Hellreigel, John W. Slocum, Jr. and Richard W. Woodman. 1992. *Organizational Behavior, Sixth Edition*. St. Paul, MN: West Publishing Company, p. 599. Reprinted by permission of the publisher. Copyright © 1992 by West Publishing Company. All rights reserved.

- The engineering and manufacturing department deals with individual customers, vendors, suppliers, and contractors.
- The marketing department deals with customers and competitors at the national and international level.
- The legal services department may deal with shareholders, courts, and regulatory agencies.
- The R&D department deals with new technology and sources of the latest scientific knowledge.[2]

Environmental characteristics. After defining the relevant project stakeholders and forces in the task environment, project managers need to assess the environmental characteristics and their relative importance to the project organization.[17] Environmental characteristics vary in terms of two major dimensions: complexity and dynamism.[2]

The complexity dimension relates to whether the environmental factors being considered are few in number and similar to each other (homogeneous) or many in number and different from each other (heterogeneous). An environment can be classified as homogenous or heterogenous on the basis of both the number of environmental factors and the number of sub-environments involved.[2] For example, the planning department of the project has a heterogeneous environment because it must consider

Organizing Projects for Success

many stakeholders and environmental factors that are continually changing. On the other hand, a production department or a quality control department faces a homogeneous environment because these departments deal with a few similar environmental factors.

The dynamism dimension relates to how much the environmental factors change. The degree of dynamism is high (i.e., projects are highly dynamic) if the factors are unstable and changing continually, as in "high-tech" industries such as the computer and communications industries. The degree of dynamism is low (i.e., projects are relatively stable) when environmental factors remain basically the same, as in conventional construction and "low-tech" industries. Project managers must continually evaluate the project organization and modify its design to respond effectively to these changes.

Task risk levels. Task environments are classified in terms of complexity and dynamism. The varying levels of complexity and dynamism interact to produce the risk level of the task environment. There are basically four types of task environment, ranging from low- to high-risk.[2]

- *A low-risk environment* is characterized by few and unchanging environmental factors, requiring a minimal level of skills and training. Essential product manufacturing is an example of a low-risk environment.

- *A moderate-risk environment* is characterized by many environmental factors, but few changes; a higher level of skills is required. Human resource departments and oil and gas refineries are moderate-risk environments.

- *A moderately high-risk environment* is characterized by few but constantly changing environmental factors. Textile, fashion, and fast-food industries are examples of this environment.

- *A high-risk environment* is characterized by many continually changing factors. Standard procedures are impractical in this environment and sophisticated problem-solving skills are needed. Basic research programs and the computer software industry are examples of high-risk environments.

The degree of risk must be analyzed and evaluated while designing the project organization. The problems and opportunities confronting most complex project organizations have become more numerous and diverse.[18] One authority has commented:

> The new managerial calculus suggests that only 20 percent of business factors are, in any sense, controllable and that 80 percent are uncontrollable. What is beyond business' control is its environment—that "buzzing, blooming, confusion" (to many managers and employees) of global, national, and business events. This environment is the source of the shocks and surprises that batter traditional business performance and make mincemeat of strategies that are inadequately attuned to these changes. [19]

Each type of task environment requires unique ways of describing and managing a project and its organization, division or department.

Strategic choices

Many of top management's strategic choices can affect organizational design of projects.[20,21] For example, three major strategic choices are:

Values and philosophy. Top management's basic values and philosophy influence the project control system and degrees of centralization and decentralization.

A philosophy of centralization requires more levels of hierarchy with more resources devoted to monitoring and controlling lower-level departments than does a decentralized design. For example, if management prefers centralization, then quality control, human resources, and auditing departments may be given larger budgets and authority than otherwise.

Type of client. What is the market segment or the client base that an organization wants to serve? For example, large firms that sell multiple lines of goods and services, such as ITT, Gulf and Western, Procter and Gamble group together the resources needed to manufacture and market each product line. Also, top management must be aware of the different requirements and concerns of the public or private client. For example, public clients are primarily concerned with the visibility, political implications and publicity aspects of the project, whereas private organizations are primarily market-oriented and are concerned with cost effectiveness, rate of return, future growth opportunities, and flexibility to cope with changes.

Where to market and produce goods and services. Where to market and produce goods and services can have a significant effect on project organizational design. For example, Allstate Insurance has a strategy to market insurance only in North America, whereas Ford Motor Company, Kodak, Sony and Xerox are interested in the global market. Consequently, they need to create much more complex organizational structures than do organizations that only manufacture and market in a particular country or region of the world. It may be desirable to integrate various projects or components of a project to focus on overall program management. Each project or part of a project may require different strategic choices to optimize the use of resources and maximize profits.

Technological factors

Work flow uncertainty, task uncertainty, and task interdependence affect job design. These three technological factors also influence organizational design, especially in terms of:
- The creation of departments or project units
- The delegation of authority and responsibility
- The need for formal integration among them.

Work flow uncertainty and task uncertainty. *Work flow uncertainty* refers to a project unit or department's degree of knowledge about when inputs will be received for processing. With low work flow uncertainty, a department has little discretion to decide which, when or where tasks will be

Table 3.1 Risk-based organizational design framework

Work Environment	Task Uncertainty	Work Flow Uncertainty
R&D, planning, or project director's unit	High	High
Investments, market research, engineering design units	High	Low
Hospital ER, fire-fighting department, power plant control room	Low	High
Conventional construction, assembly line	Low	Low

performed.[2] *Task uncertainty* refers to the extent of a project unit's well-defined knowledge about how to perform the tasks assigned to it.[22] Low task uncertainty implies that members of the unit generally know how to perform the task and produce desired outcomes. A high task uncertainty situation requires that key members of the project unit apply their experience, judgment, and intuition and jointly define and solve problems in order to achieve the desired project goals.

As the levels of work flow uncertainty and task uncertainty interact and fluctuate from low to high, four basic types of work environment are created, as shown in Table 3.1. For example, R&D departments and planning departments are generally characterized by high task uncertainty and high work flow uncertainty (especially during scope definition and commissioning). On the other hand, in a conventional construction project, the technology is well-known and the work flow can be easily projected. Consequently, both the task uncertainty and work flow uncertainty is low. It is desirable to keep both the task uncertainty and work flow uncertainty low, which can be done through better planning and proper training. By redesigning the project organization, most project units can be modified to alter the task uncertainty and work flow uncertainty.

Departments may be formed on the basis of similarities in technological characteristics. Functional departments can contribute resources for any project in the organization as needed to meet workloads throughout the project life cycle.

Task interdependence. Task interdependence refers to the degree of interdependency between the tasks of various project units. Three types of task interdependence are:[2]

Pooled interdependence occurs when each project unit is relatively autonomous and makes an identifiable contribution towards project goals. For example, the local sales and marketing departments of a computer manufacturing organization (such as IBM or Apple.) are interdependent on headquarters that coordinate the development and release of new hardware/software products and set policies and prices.

Sequential interdependence occurs when one project unit must complete certain tasks before one or more other project units can perform their tasks. For example, in a manufacturing project environment, the design department provides its output to the fabrication department, which in turn provides its output to the assembly department and then to the painting, finishing, and so on.

Reciprocal interdependence occurs when outputs of one project unit become the inputs for another and resulting output becomes input for the first project, and so on. For example, planning, marketing, and R&D departments at AT&T are likely to have many reciprocal interdependencies in the development of new telecommunication services.

Reciprocal interdependence is the most complex type, whereas pooled interdependence is the simplest type of task interdependence. Greater interdependence requires greater integration of departments. Placing reciprocally interdependent project units under a common manager often improves communication and integration and minimizes information processing costs. For example, the marketing research, advertising, and sales departments may report to the vice president of marketing. Project participants in these departments must communicate and coordinate more with each other than with people in the maintenance department.

Information technologies have considerable influence on the jobs of many people. These technologies also have a significant impact on the design of many project organizations and on the flow of information through them.[23] For example, most computer manufacturers now use computer-based information technologies to improve their ability to manage numerous task interdependencies.

Summary

Organizing is a key element of project management. It determines the major tasks to be performed, the jobs or positions required to complete the tasks, and the resources needed to accomplish the tasks and meet the project objectives. It is directly related to planning and therefore must be considered at the outset to start the project on the right foot. Organizing is the process of establishing effective use of all project resources in order to accomplish the project objectives. It assists project managers not only in setting project goals and milestones but also in clarifying which resources will be needed to attain them with minimum unintended problems and conflicts.

It is important to understand the importance of organizing, the seven-step organizing process, the organizing subsystem, and the four dimensions (formalization, centralization, complexity, and specialization) of organizational structure that must be analyzed to design an organization for any project. Some widely known classic organizational principles such as unity of command, parity in authority and responsibility, chain of command, span of management and control, flexibility, division of labor, and departmentation should be used in organizing a project.

In addition to just designing an organizational structure that shows authority and reporting relationships, organizational design strategies must emphasize how to make the organization really work. The seven-step organizing process should be continually updated and active feedback should be genuinely sought to optimize the effectiveness and efficiency of all stakeholders as individuals and as project teams. In order to design practical, effective project organizations, the roles and relationship between formalization, centralization, specialization and complexity should be analyzed, evaluated and implemented carefully to fit the situation, nature of the project, project teams, other stakeholders and top management.

The design of an appropriate project organization is a complex process. It is heavily influenced by several factors. There are three major factors: environmental forces (task and overall organizational environment), strategic choices (values and philosophy of top management and type of clients), and technological factors. The task environment(s) in a project as a whole and in its various units can vary greatly. Project managers must consider the combined effects of these forces in order to design a project organization which facilitates teamwork, effective communication, easy and smooth flow of information and decision making to satisfy clients and other project stakeholders and optimize the creative potential of everyone involved in the project. They must develop organizational design strategies to fit the needs of the project according to its size, complexity, human dynamics, and overall culture of the organization.

Barbara A. Maino

chapter

Outline

4

98

In spite of the best-laid plans, projects often fail because project managers don't have the right structures in place.

4

Important Issues in Project Organizational Design

A LTHOUGH PROJECT MANAGEMENT concepts are simple, their application can be very complex, whether they are being applied to an existing organization or to a newly-organized project. Ineptly conceived or poorly executed project management concepts lead to failure. The most traumatic aspect of implementing project management is the reorganization or realignment of an existing organization. Changes within an organization (especially shifts in authority) cause conflict and tension. And every project will have a unique form of project management that changes throughout the project life cycle, causing more potentially controversial organizational change.

The fact that project managers have enormous responsibility and accountability along with limited authority poses interesting challenges. They may have to delegate project activities that they cannot do themselves because of heavy workload or the technical skills required. They must determine to whom to delegate, and then delegate effectively. They must assign responsibility, grant appropriate authority, expect reliability, and require accountability from the delegatees. The issues of accountability and reliability become even more important when project personnel are assigned responsibilities critical to project success.

Project managers must design their project organizations by analyzing and evaluating the issues of responsibility, authority, reliability, and accountability and by balancing these to optimize human interactions with minimum barriers. They must be able to organize the project participants and their activities in a manner that facilitates open communication, successful delegation, and effective team building. ∎

Authority, Responsibility, Accountability, and Reliability

Reliability and accountability exist only when sufficient authority is granted to fulfill a responsibility.

Project management is becoming recognized as a useful and effective management tool in all industries. Since productivity results from the specific activities performed by various individuals within the organization, organizing a project should include not just a rationale for an orderly use of resources, but also four key elements of organizing that specifically channel the efforts of project participants. These four elements—authority, accountability, responsibility, and reliability—are like the four legs of a stool, as shown in Figure 4.1. Because these elements are critical for the flow of work to proceed smoothly, they must be in balance in order to be effective. Briefly,

- *Authority* confers the right to impose some degree of obedience.
- *Responsibility* confers the obligation on the recipient to act with or without detailed guidance or specific authorization.
- *Reliability* refers to the degree to which the recipient of authority and responsibility can be depended upon, i.e., to respond with sound and consistent effort.
- *Accountability* in the project context is the extent to which the individual or team of individuals are answerable and must provide visible evidence of their actions.

These four elements are highly interrelated. For example,

- When authority is granted to someone, accountability must be required; and
- When responsibility is assigned, reliability to accomplish must be expected.

These interrelationships should be understood in order to justify giving rewards or recognition to motivate participants.

Therefore, authority and responsibility (which refers to acting and accomplishing) must be balanced by an appropriate level of accountability and reliability (which refers to accomplishing and then deserving proper rewards or recognition). In other words, people can be held accountable only if proper authority and responsibility are given and if they get appropriate recognition/rewards for fulfilling their responsibilities. This dynamic is illustrated in Figure 4.2.

Authority

Authority is the right to perform or command, the right to make a decision or to perform a specific action that will affect the organization. Authority is a conceptual framework and, at the same time, an enigma in the study of organizations.[1] It is usually defined as a legal or rightful power to command others to act or not to act.

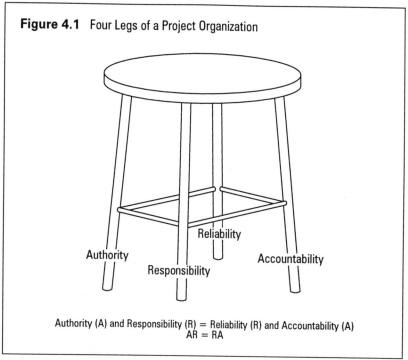

Figure 4.1 Four Legs of a Project Organization

Reliability

Authority

Responsibility

Accountability

Authority (A) and Responsibility (R) = Reliability (R) and Accountability (A)
$$AR = RA$$

Source: R.M. Wideman. January 1995. Personal Communication.

Early theories of manpower regarded authority as a gravitational force that flowed from the top down. However, recent theories emphasize that authority is a force that must be accepted voluntarily and that acts both horizontally and vertically. In the traditional theory of management, authority is a right granted from a superior to a subordinate. Authority increases the probability that a specific command will be obeyed, yet for the command to be obeyed, authority must be *granted* by the manager and *accepted* by the subordinate.

In order to develop practical techniques for using authority effectively in the project environment, one must have an understanding of the various types of authority and how they relate to projects.

Project authority. Authority is essential to any group or project team effort. Project management structures create complex relationships that can lead to problems in the delegation of authority and the internal authority structure. Four questions that must be considered in describing project authority are:[2]

• What is project authority?
• What is power and how is it achieved?
• How much project authority should be given to the project manager?

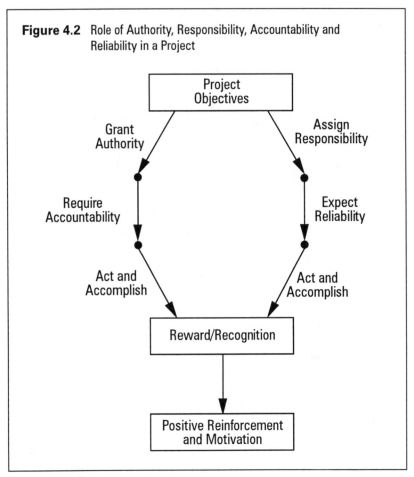

Figure 4.2 Role of Authority, Responsibility, Accountability and Reliability in a Project

Project Objectives

Grant Authority

Assign Responsibility

Require Accountability

Expect Reliability

Act and Accomplish

Act and Accomplish

Reward/Recognition

Positive Reinforcement and Motivation

Source: R.M. Wideman. January 1995. Personal Communication.

- Who settles project authority interface problems?

Two main sources of authority are:[1]

Personal or formal authority (*de jure* project authority) is derived from position in the organization. This legal authority of a project manager usually is contained in some form of documentation, which also contains the complementary roles of other managers (e.g., functional managers, work package managers, and general managers) associated with the project.

Informal or earned authority is acquired on the basis of the knowledge, skills, abilities, and personal effectiveness. It is also called *de facto* project authority.[1]

Figure 4.3 shows a project-functional organizational interface that can be viewed as a model for prescribing the relative authority exercised by

Organizing Projects for Success

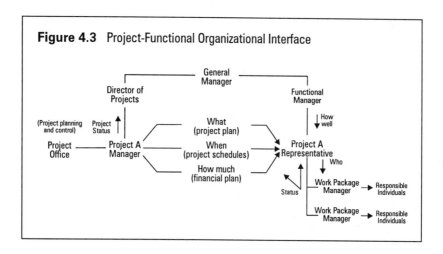

Figure 4.3 Project-Functional Organizational Interface

project managers in the matrix organization in which they share responsibility with the functional managers for allocating resources and assigning priorities. In this model, which is based on the assumption that each participant has the authority to carry out all his or her assigned responsibilities, the tasks of the project are divided as follows:

The Director of Projects matches projects to the appropriate project managers; directs and evaluates those managers' activities; plans, proposes and implements project management methodology and policies; and ensures project compliance with contractual commitments.

The Functional Manager accomplishes work package tasks on schedule and within budget; provides functional policy and procedural guidance; provides adequately skilled staff; and maintains technical excellence.

The Project Manager develops and maintains project scope, budgets, and schedules; negotiates with functional managers for use of the required resources; directs and integrates project activities; and evaluates and reports project performance.

The Project Representative within the functional department is a key individual, the focal point of all activity on a project, performing all subfunctional tasking. Such a representative, who is required to interface between the project manager, the functional manager, and the work package manager, needs to possess good interpersonal skills as well as political savvy.

The Work Package Managers develop and maintain work package plans; establish work package technical guidance, detailed schedules, and operating budgets; and control and report work package performance.[1]

TODAY, A PROJECT MANAGER MUST LEARN to manage his or her projects by using informal authority. Formal authority should be used only when necessary. In the traditional structure, power is realized through the management hierarchy, whereas in the project structure, power comes from credibility, knowledge, expertise, and from being a sound decision maker.

Types of authority. Authority can be of many types, depending upon the job or position of individuals.

Line authority is the right to give orders and make decisions concerning the end product, sales, etc. It reflects existing manager-subordinate relationships. Generally, project managers (especially in a projectized or strong matrix environment) may have line authority over the personnel working on their projects but only for the duration of the project or assigned task, because individuals return to their respective functional departments as soon as their work is complete.

Because line authority maintains a simple chain of command and a clear division of authority and accountability, it is advantageous in situations where speedy decision making and action are required. However, it has disadvantages in that it neglects the input of specialists in the planning phase and overworks key people, who thus become nearly indispensable and, at the same time, more at risk of burnout.

Staff authority is the right to advise and assist those who have line authority. It should be considered a service function, aimed at improving the effectiveness of line personnel in performing their required tasks. Line and staff personnel must work together to improve overall efficiency and effectiveness. Examples of personnel with staff authority associated with a project are accountants, lawyers, and personnel managers. There is a stronger need for staff personnel on large projects. For example, large and complex international projects may need advice on financing, negotiating, satisfying regulatory agencies, and industrial relations issues.

Staff authority has advantages in that it enables specialists to give expert advice, while freeing the line executive from detailed analysis. On the downside, it can confuse the organization's chain of command if functions are not clearly assigned. It also undermines the authority of experts if they have the responsibility to provide input without the authority to put their recommendations into action. In an organization relying on staff authority, power tends to be more centralized, which inhibits the implementation of empowerment strategies.

Note: Conflict may arise between line and staff personnel when staff personnel assume line authority, do not give sound advice, do not keep line personnel informed, or steal credit for success. Overcoming these conflicts requires serious and continuous watchfulness. On the other hand, line personnel can minimize conflict by using staff personnel wherever possible, making proper use of staff expertise, and keeping them informed. Figure 4.4 shows a typical line/staff relationship in a project environment.[3]

Functional authority is the right to give orders within a particular segment of the organization. It generally covers only specific task areas and is

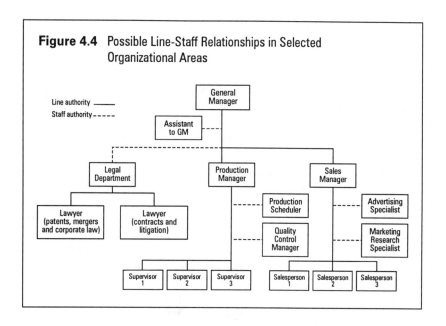

Figure 4.4 Possible Line-Staff Relationships in Selected Organizational Areas

valid for as long as the person holds that position. Relying on functional authority relieves line executives of routine, specialized decisions; provides a framework for applying expert knowledge; and limits the need for "jack-of-all-trades" executives. However, such authority makes intra-organizational relationships more complex, in that it becomes difficult to coordinate and set boundaries for the authority of each functional specialist. Therefore, power tends to be more centralized. Often, line, staff, and functional authority can be combined for the overall benefit of the organization.

Authority versus power. The terms *authority* and *power* are frequently confused. As defined earlier, authority is the right to command and is generally granted based on one's position in the organizational hierarchy. Power, on the other hand, is the ability or capacity to influence the actions or decisions of others without necessarily having formal authority. Authority can be considered as a part of the larger concept of power. Formal authority, which is gained by one's formal position or status in the organization, is just one of the means by which an individual can have some power and thereby influence others.

Project managers should be aware of this difference between authority and power in managing politics at the top management level as well as at the project level. There may be some members in the organization who may not have very much formal authority but may have considerable power to influence because of their scarce and important specialized skills, high technical expertise, or ownership of the organization. Project managers must be aware of such situations when organizing their projects.

Important Issues in Project Organizational Design

Sources of power. In addition to positional or formal authority, project managers may use power and influence available from several sources. French and Raven[4] developed five basic categories of power:

Legitimate power is the formal authority of the project manager, i.e., the right to give orders or make requests. The legitimate power of the project manager is determined by the norms, perceptions, and expectations of project personnel. For example, "Has the project manager done this before?", "Have project personnel always complied?" and "What are the consequences of noncompliance?"

Coercive power or punishment power refers to negative things that project personnel believe a project manager can do to them—fire, suspend, dock pay, give unpleasant assignments, or reprimand.

Reward power refers to positive consequences or outcomes that a project manager can offer to project personnel. It includes positive incentives such as promotions, salary increases, vacations and other opportunities.

Referent power refers to the earned or personal power that accrues to a project manager when project personnel admire him or her as a person. This mainly comes about because of the project manager's personal qualities. In such situations, personnel willingly comply with the demands of their project manager, whom they look up to as a role model.

Expert power is also an earned or personal power, acquired on the basis of technical knowledge, skill, and expertise on some topic or issue. In such situations, project personnel will do what the project manager wants because they believe that the project manager knows best. Expert power is a function of knowledge and skills possessed by the project manager rather than of formal organizational status.

The various forms of power are interrelated and do overlap. The dynamics of power are very complicated. Youker has identified some interesting ideas about various forms of power.[5]

- Some forms of power are derived from formal authority, while some are personal or earned and come from the individual (charisma).
- People may have direct power or indirect power through someone else (contacts).
- Power may be used or not.
- In fact, people can have power only if others perceive it that way.

For the project manager who wishes to use the power effectively, two factors are important:

1. *Appropriate choice of power base* may depend upon the situation and the maturity level of the project manager.
2. *Skillful and thoughtful execution of power* is the most important aspect because better interpersonal and persuasive skills, combined with effective communication and positive reinforcement, will result in better influence (compared to an autocratic style).

Some practical suggestions about project authority. Generally, project managers have considerable responsibility but limited authority. The amount of authority granted to project managers should depend upon project size, management philosophy, and level of priority in comparison to ongoing functional activities. However, they must be tactful, diplomatic, and use their authority appropriately. Some important points about authority in a project environment are:[2]

1. *The project manager must have sufficient authority to control the project effectively.* According to Steiner and Ryan:

   On a large project, the project manager should have broad authority over all elements of the project. His authority should be sufficient to permit him to engage in all necessary managerial and technical actions required to complete the project successfully. He should have appropriate authority for designing and making technical decisions with the proper support and advice from technical experts. He should be able to control funds, schedule and quality of product. If subcontractors are used, he should have sufficient authority in their selection process.[6]

2. *The higher the risk, the more authority should be granted to the project manager.* Project managers in matrix structures should have more authority than functional managers. Where the project managers only have monitoring authority, they are really operating in a weak matrix with staff authority as project coordinators or project expediters.

3. *Project managers must organize the projects appropriately in terms of authority relationships.* Failure to establish proper authority relationships can result in:[2]
   - Poor communication
   - Misleading information
   - Opposition, especially from the informal organization
   - Poor working relationships with superiors, subordinates, peers, and associates
   - Surprises for the customer.

Although authority often depends upon personal abilities and experience, project managers can further strengthen their position by documenting project authority.

Documentation. Good project managers should know the boundaries of their authority, and documentation of project authority can help in establishing these boundaries. Project authority can be expressed in policy manuals, policy letters, and standard operating procedures. These sources should delineate the project manager's role and prerogatives with regard to:[1]

Establishing clear authority and responsibility relationships among the project manager, functional managers, task managers, and general managers, which encompass:

- The project manager's focus on project activities
- The need for influence that cuts across functional and organizational lines to achieve unanimity on the project objective
- Active participation in major management and technical decisions required to complete the project
- Rights in resolving conflicts that jeopardize project goals
- Participation in the merit evaluation of key project personnel.[7]

Establishing authority to organize the project for success by:
- Establishing an appropriate project organizational design for the duration of the project
- Having a voice in maintaining the integrity of the project team during the complete life of the project
- Providing an information system for the project with sufficient data for control of the project within allowable cost, schedule, and technical parameters
- Maintaining prime customer liaison and contact on project matters.

Establishing authority to control project resources (external and internal) by:
- Establishing project plans through the coordinated efforts of the organizations involved in the project
- Collaborating (with personnel office and functional supervisors) in staffing the project
- Selection of subcontractors and negotiation of contracts
- Control over the allocation and expenditure of funds and active participation in major budgeting and scheduling deliberations.

Documentation of project authority also assists senior management in encouraging the acceptance of project goals and management priorities by others in power. Such documentation:
- Provides leadership in the preparation of operational requirements, specifications, justifications, and the bid package
- Promotes technological and managerial improvements throughout the life of the project
- Manages the cost, schedule, and technical performance parameters of the project[6]
- Clarifies expectations regarding reliability and accountability in response to authority and responsibility among the project manager, functional managers, task managers, and general managers.

Ideally, project managers should try to manage their projects by using informal (earned) authority because it helps gain more respect, trust, and hence commitment in the long run. When they have to use their formal authority, it should be done only as a last resort. In any case, project managers must exercise their authority in a diplomatic and tactful manner through effective communication and negotiating strategies.

Authority is essential to any group or project team effort. The project manager's authority provides the cohesive force for the project team. It is important to understand the elements of project authority and the complex authority relationships in a project structure, which must be developed with caution. Conflicts between line staff and functional managers may at times occur and should be resolved immediately before these conflicts start affecting project performance.

Authority operates in the context of responsibility, reliability, and accountability as shown in Figure 4.1.

Responsibility

The price of greatness is responsibility.

— *Winston Churchill*

Responsibility, the second leg of our four-legged stool (authority, responsibility, reliability, and accountability), is a significant issue in managing a project. Responsibility represents an obligation to perform an assigned activity with or without detailed guidance or specific authorization. It is a self-assumed commitment to handle the job to the best of one's ability. Authority and responsibility must go hand in hand. In a project environment, a responsible person must be legally and/or ethically answerable (accountable) for meeting project objectives consistent with organizational policies and procedures, and for the welfare of project participants, the project, and the whole organization. Responsibility implies having the ability to make rational decisions, to be trusted to make such decisions, and to be held accountable for those decisions.

Responsibility is an obligation that a person accepts, and ultimate responsibility cannot be delegated or passed on to someone else in the project. Even though project managers are responsible for planning, controlling and evaluating all project activities, they cannot perform all these duties on their own. The project manager must learn to delegate and divide work appropriately among the various members of the project team and integrate the efforts of project engineer, project contractors, cost administrator, support services, etc. Nevertheless, project managers are still ultimately responsible for tasks delegated to others. Consequently, they must make sure that the delegatees are reliable (i.e., they will produce quality results) and that they are held accountable.

Major issues of responsibility. Because responsibility is a complex issue, any ambiguities can lead to serious project problems. In most projects, there are three major issues related to responsibility.[8]

Dividing job activities. Typically, many people are involved in a project; a single person cannot complete all the activities alone. Therefore, it is important to devise a method of distributing project activities and channeling the activities of the participants. After identifying project objectives, activities with similar functions are grouped by developing a work

Important Issues in Project Organizational Design

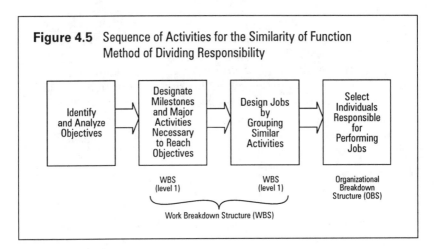

Figure 4.5 Sequence of Activities for the Similarity of Function Method of Dividing Responsibility

breakdown structure and an organizational breakdown structure, using four interrelated sequential steps as shown in Figure 4.5. This is one of the most basic methods of dividing the whole project into smaller and more manageable activities, or work packages. Managers should avoid overlapping responsibility, allowing responsibility gaps, and defining job activities that do not enhance the attainment of project objectives.[9]

Clarifying job activities of project managers. Because the project manager plays a pivotal role, clarification of his or her job is a key factor in meeting the project objectives within time, cost and quality constraints. Project managers must interact with top management, functional managers, peers, and project team personnel (subordinates). A management responsibility guide as shown in Figure 4.6 can be used to implement this interaction.[10]

This management responsibility guide can assist project personnel in describing various project responsibility relationships and in summarizing how these relationships relate to each other within the project.

Being responsible. Project team members can be described as *responsible* if they are *reliable*, i.e., they can be trusted to perform the activities they are assigned to perform.[11] Project managers have the maximum impact on project performance and success. Responsible and reliable behavior by project managers is valued highly by clients and top management in the organization, if they direct individuals in performing their project duties efficiently and effectively. The degree of responsibility possessed by project managers can be assessed by their:[12]

- *Attitude towards and conduct with project team members.* Responsible project managers work interdependently and in harmony, producing and planning collectively. They provide direction, challenge and support their teams, and give praise and recognition as well as constructive criticism, thereby maintaining morale and productivity. They stay on top of activities and problems, as well as change and growth among

110

Figure 4.6 Seven Responsibility Relationships Between Managers

1. General Responsibility	Refers to guiding and directing the execution of work packages through the persons accepting operating responsibility
2. Operating Responsibility	Refers to the responsibility for executing the assigned work package
3. Specific Responsibility	Refers to executing a specific or limited portion of the work package
4. Must Be Consulted	Relevant stakeholders that must be called upon before any decision is made or approval is granted to render advice or information. However, they may not make the actual decision or grant approval (e.g. vendors, contractors, client)
5. May Be Consulted	Relevant stakeholders may be called upon to relate information, render advice, or make recommendations (e.g.. vendors, contractors, appropriate team members)
6. Must Be Notified	Relevant stakeholders must be notified of actions that have been taken (e.g. client, regulatory authorities)
7. Must Approve	The individual(s) who must approve or disapprove, other than persons holding general and operating responsibility (e.g. client and senior management)

Adapted from: Robert D. Melcher. 1967. Roles and Relationships: Clarifying the Manager's Job. *Personnel,* 44 (May/June): pp. 35, 38–39. © 1967, American Management Association, New York, NY. Reprinted by permission of the publisher.

team members, thus providing leadership suited to the situation and the maturity level of their teams.

- *Behavior with top management.* Responsible project managers ensure that their teams meet the project's objectives and, in the process, satisfy the expectations of the client and upper management.
- *Behavior with other project managers and functional managers.* Responsible project managers ensure that interfaces between the project team, internal stakeholders, and external stakeholders are managed effectively and ethically.
- *Personal attitudes and values.* Responsible project managers identify with their project team, performing tasks that help the team and/or the organization. They think of themselves more as coaches and facilitators than as commanders or controllers. Their personal values are congruent with the goals of the organization and the project, which enables them to "walk their talk" and lessens conflicts between their personal desires and project activities.

Typical charter of program or project manager (in a matrix organization). A charter for a project manager should clearly describe authority and responsibilities. A charter assists in the selection of a project manager; once it is designed for the project, it must be accepted by the client, project team members, and functional managers in order for a project organization to be functionally effective. It is essential for managers on large projects and programs. It should be pointed out that charters for project managers or program managers are very similar to each other except that program managers may be managing several projects. A typical charter for a program or project manager in a matrix organization clearly establishes the responsibility and authority of project manager as in the following model:[13]

Responsibility of the project manager. The project manager is responsible to the client and to top management for meeting project objectives within specified constraints of cost, schedule, and quality or technical performance. More specifically, the project manager is responsible for:

- *Preparing and maintaining the project plan* includes master schedules, budgets, technical and performance specifications, scope and statements of work, work breakdown structure, and procedure for task authorizations and change orders. Planning should be done in collaboration with the client, key vendors/suppliers, and project team members to gain their acceptance and hence commitment to the project plan. The project plan should be viewed as a "live" document, i.e., it should be updated regularly.

- *Organizing the project* includes identifying functional resources required to do the activities shown on the work breakdown structure, matching skills with resources, establishing reporting relationships, and authorizing performance. Project organizational design should facilitate communication and enhance teamwork. This step of assigning appropriate resources is commonly called Organizational Breakdown Structure.

- *Managing the project*—achieving project objectives within specified constraints through effective management and control of project activities and resources—includes interfacing with all stakeholders, coordinating and integrating efforts of all project team members, contractors, subcontractors, vendors, and support personnel. To manage the project successfully, project managers must have good interpersonal skills, including communication, motivation, leadership, negotiation, problemsolving, decision making, and conflict management. Any problems and deficiencies should be identified, evaluated, and resolved to avoid undesirable effects on the schedule, budget, and quality of the project.

- *Communicating the project status and projecting the completion date* involves establishing and maintaining appropriate communication channels among the client, top management, and project team members. Communication breakdown is one of the main reasons for project failures. Project managers should choose appropriate tools and styles to facilitate communication about project status and projected completion date. These include status meetings, design reviews, periodic overall project reviews, monitoring of budgets and schedules, and progress reports from key areas. In addition to just reporting the project status, project managers should identify problems and make suggestions to resolve them.

- *Post-project audit and summary.* In addition to satisfying all reviews and acceptance requirements, project managers must transfer the product or facility, train client personnel, prepare final reports and accounts, and close out records. They must participate in any post-project audits or postmortem analysis in order to analyze deficiencies and learn lessons that will improve their future performance on other projects.

The first responsibility (planning) requires more emphasis on leadership skills to clearly establish the client's needs and define the "right things to do" (effectiveness), whereas the last three responsibilities require more emphasis on managership skills and focus on "doing things right" (efficiency).

Authority of the project manager. Project managers cannot fulfill their responsibilities without sufficient authority being given by higher management. Project managers are typically authorized to:
- Direct all program activities
- Act as a representative of the organization in contacts with the client, internal stakeholders, and external stakeholders
- Negotiate with contractors, lenders, suppliers, etc.
- Approve all assignments, expenditures, and change orders.

Project managers acquire informal authority on the basis of their knowledge, skills, and special expertise. Informal authority increases their professional credibility and enhances their ability to influence project stakeholders to meet project objectives successfully.

In matrix structures, the responsibilities and authority between project managers and functional managers are not crystal clear, which may lead to difficulties. However, preparing a project charter at the front end may help alleviate some of those problems by clarifying the responsibilities and authority of project managers. In most cases, program charters can be prepared using a similar model to that of a project charter, with the exception that a program typically encompasses several interrelated projects.

Responsibilities of project manager and functional managers. Assuming that the project manager and the line managers are different persons, two major responsibilities of functional managers are:[14]
1. To define *how* the task will be done and *where* it will be done (i.e., the technical criteria); and
2. To provide sufficient trained and competent resources to meet project objectives within constraints, i.e., *who* will get the job done (managerial personnel) and *who* will actually do the job (technical personnel).

Project management does not always follow the principle of *unity of command*. Projects are often designed with shared authority and responsibility between the project managers and functional managers. The project managers plan, monitor, and control the project whereas the functional managers are responsible for doing the work. Figure 4.7 shows this shared responsibility.

Important Issues in Project Organizational Design

Figure 4.7 Typical Responsibilities of the Functional and Project
Managers

Project Activity	Responsibilities	
	Project Manager	**Functional Manager**
Plan	Seeks input and prepares a project plan	Executes the work packages according to project plan
Organize	Seeks input, matches resources/responsibility	Agrees and provides resources
Execution/Direction	Active on a regular basis, emphasis on integration	Supervision as required and liaisons with project manager
Monitor/Control	Emphasis on overall (macro)	Emphasis on details (micro)
Evaluate/Give	Overall (summary)	Detailed
Reward/Recognize	Recommends	Provides rewards

Adapted from: Harold Kerzner. 1989. *Project Management: A Systems Approach to Planning, Scheduling and Controlling. Third Edition.* New York, NY: Van Nostrand Reinhold, p.16. Reprinted by permission of the publisher.

It may create a conflict of interest when a functional manager is also the project manager. By saving the best resources for a portion of the project that he or she is directly responsible for, a functional manager/project manager may achieve success in one area at the expense of failure in others. For this reason, although functional managers do sometimes serve as project managers, this may not be the best approach for the overall health of the organization.

Linear responsibility chart. Kocaoglu and Cleland developed a linear responsibility chart[15] that is very useful for clarifying the responsibilities of all those involved in a project because the traditional organizational chart has some general disadvantages:

• It does not establish relationships between position and work.
• It lacks specificity.
• There is a lack of dialogue in its preparation, and consequently, a lack of commitment to make it work.
• It does not show reciprocal team member roles.

Developing a Linear Responsibility Chart (LRC) is a practical approach to designing a project organization because it goes beyond a simple display of formal lines of communication, gradations of organization level, departmentalization, and line-staff relationships. It is very similar in concept to a responsibility matrix. An LRC reveals the interfaces between work packages and organizational positions. Figure 4.8 shows a typical LRC for a project-driven organization.

114

Figure 4.8 Sample Linear Responsibility Chart

Work Packages	Contract Admin.	Mfg. Manager	Financial Manager	Profit Ctr. Division Manager	R&D Manager	Marketing Manager	Mgt. Council	Comments
Settings corporate objectives	I, O	I, O	I, O	I, O	I, O	I, O	P	
Developing Corp. Maint. agreements	P	N	I, N	I, A		I, N		
Negotiating customer contracts	I, R	I, N	R	P			A	
New product development		I, O	I	I*, O	P	I*, R		
Developing bid strategies	I, O	I, O		I, O		P	A	
Preparing the annual budget	I, O	I, O	P	I, O	I, O	I, O		
Developing master schedule for opers.	N	P	N	I, N	I, N			
Establishing standard costs		W	P	I, O				

Legend:

P–Primary Responsiblity–the prime authority and responsibility for accomplishment of work package
R–Review–reviews output of work package
N–Notification–is notified of output of work package
A–Approval–approves work package
O–Output–receives output of work package
I*–Initiation–initiates work package

I–Input–provides input to work package
W–Work is Done–accomplishes actual labor of work package
P includes W
P includes A
P includes I*
A includes R
Unless otherwise specified

Source: D.F. Kocaoglu and D.I. Cleland. 1983. The RIM Process: A Participative Approach to the Development of Organizational Roles and Interactions. *Management Review* (October): p. 61. ©1983 American Management Association. Reprinted by permission of the publisher. All rights reserved.

Developing the LRC is a process that helps people understand how they relate to the organizational work packages. This process is as important as the product (the completed LRC). Once developed, the LRC becomes a model for the intended formal relationships in the project. Also, the LRC can become a "living document" used to:

- Portray formal authority, responsibility, and accountability relationships
- Acquaint newcomers with how things are done in the organization
- Get people committed and motivated so that they know what is expected of them
- Bring out real or potential conflict over territorial prerogatives in the organization
- Permit people to see the "big picture"—how they fit into the larger whole
- Facilitate teamwork, because people have a greater opportunity to see their role on the team
- Provide a standard against which the project manager can monitor productivity.

Six key elements that make up the form and process of an LRC are:

1. An organizational position
2. An element of work—a work package—that must be accomplished to support organizational objectives and strategies
3. An organizational interface point—a common boundary of action between an organizational position and a work package
4. A legend describing the specificity of the organizational interface
5. A procedure for designing, developing, and operating LRCs for an organization.
6. Commitment and dedication on the part of members of the organization to make the LRC process work.

An LRC can assist project managers in understanding their authority relationships with other players. Figure 4.8 shows an LRC for project-functional management relationships within a matrix organization.[15] The development of such a chart, combined with the discussions that accompany such development, can help a great deal in facilitating an understanding of project management and how it will affect the day-to-day work of project team members.

Responsibility represents an obligation to perform the tasks assigned, according to one's best ability. Generally, responsibilities in a project environment are derived from job descriptions of the project participant and from their formal roles within the organization. The effectiveness of most project organizations depends on how effectively the project manager and other project participants fulfill their responsibilities towards the accomplishment of project objectives while also meeting their personal goals. The development of an LRC and clarification of responsibilities of project personnel can greatly contribute to achieving this and also contribute towards creating an environment that fosters teamwork. It is useful to review individual responsibilities and how they relate to those of others in the project on an ongoing basis and make any adjustments as necessary throughout the project life cycle.

Reliability

Reliability is the third leg of our four-legged stool. In general, a recipient of authority and responsibility is said to be reliable when he or she is worthy of confidence and can be trusted. Reliability refers not only to moral qualities but also to judgment, knowledge, skill, and habit,[16] and implies that one is willing to put one's best efforts into accomplishing the assigned tasks. In a project environment, reliability refers to the degree to which a project participant who is given certain responsibility and authority will contribute sound, consistent, and best effort to complete the assigned task within the specified constraints of time, budget, and quality.

Reliability encompasses two main factors—*track record* and *quality of work.*

Reliability and track record. Like motivation, reliability comes from within. Some project participants feel personally obligated to perform the tasks assigned to them. They are self-disciplined and don't have to be forced to accept responsibility. They do their best because of personal pride. Project managers can rely upon these people, because they have a good solid track record of delivering what they promise. In a project environment, personnel are assigned to the project from a variety of functional departments and project managers may not have a direct knowledge about their degree of reliability. Also, project managers do not and need not have enough time to closely supervise and monitor the progress of everyone involved in the project. However, they are dependent upon the successful completion of project tasks assigned to their people. Under such circumstances, it is important that the project personnel be highly reliable and that they can be fully trusted to fulfill their assigned responsibilities. This kind of self-discipline, which enhances reliability of project personnel, is not only good but essential for organizing and managing the projects successfully. A solid track record also usually increases one's informal authority and ability to influence others.

Project managers would normally prefer to delegate important tasks only to those who are reliable and who have track records of producing quality results. Since project teams consist of people with a diverse mix of backgrounds who are allocated to the project from various functional departments, and since project managers do not have the resources (due to time and budget constraints) to train every team members they must rely on the team members' track records. The success of the project therefore depends on the individual team members' reliability, as measured by their track records in completing challenging assignments.

Reliability and quality. Projects are organized to produce a unique product or a service through a diverse mix of project team members. Responsibilities are divided among numerous project personnel. Some are responsible for engineering and technical activities, while others are responsible for project management and project administrative activities. Project managers must integrate the efforts of all project personnel to meet project objectives. The project managers face a traditional dilemma of working effectively within a project organization where they have total responsibility and total accountability but limited authority.[17] They must rely upon the accuracy and quality of work produced by other project personnel. They need reliable people who are self-motivated and committed to produce consistent, accurate, and quality results.

In addition to the issues of authority and responsibility, the importance of reliability to produce quality results should not be overlooked in designing project organizational structures. Project managers must design project organizations in a way that facilitates communications, emphasizes quality, and enables everyone to do their best and work together as a team. In a team environment project participants work interdependently, rather than independently, which fosters human synergy and increases overall performance of project human resources.

Project personnel will not shy away from accepting accountability for their assignments if they are given opportunities to improve their skills and confidence to meet high quality standards. They will feel comfortable in accepting responsibilities if they can enhance their own reliability in producing quality results consistently and continually and can also rely on others to do the same. When delegating a responsibility and authority, the delegator expects reliability from the delegatee and the delegatee should respond by demonstrating a reliable behavior by producing quality results. When the delegator recognizes and rewards the delegatee for good performance, it leads to increased motivation and commitment to quality.

Accountability

Accountability is the fourth leg of our four-legged stool. Very often, tasks in a project environment have to be delegated. While delegating, the delegator must grant sufficient authority to fulfill the assignment and, if accepted, the delegatee should be accountable for completing the assigned task. Both the delegator and the delegatee must recognize the "accountability" aspect of this delegation process. This makes accountability an important concern in project management.

Accountability includes the acceptance of success or failure. It implies assuming a liability for a task or something of value assigned in a project through a contract or because of assigned responsibility. It relies having a serious conception of professional integrity and liability.[17] Accountability is having to answer to someone for actions performed. It reflects a measure of just how responsible project personnel are or have been.

Project managers generally have dual accountability. They are accountable to higher management for achieving excellence and to the client for managing the project in terms of its objectives of scope, quality, time, and cost. This accountability is based on their own performance and on the performance of project team members. In addition to project team members, the project managers depend on the cooperation of functional managers and other support/service personnel associated with the project. In all cases, the project managers are normally held accountable for the effectiveness and efficiency of the people who report directly or indirectly to them.

Accountability to one or more persons. Accountability can rest with a single person (a project manager) or a group of individuals such as self-directed work teams, with several executives such as top management, a management council, or a board of directors.[13] Top management integrates decision making and implementation of strategies. Specific authority, responsibility, reliability, and accountability of plural executives depends upon the size and complexity of projects. In the case of projects organized in matrix fashion,

118

authority, responsibility, reliability, and accountability are the cohesive forces that hold the project organization together and facilitate the attainment of project objectives in terms of cost, schedule, and technical performance. The degree of completeness of authority, responsibility, reliability, and accountability at each hierarchy level in the organization can influence any or all of the parameters and affect the cost, schedule, and technical performance objectives of the project.

Accountability implies rewards and punishments. The concept of accountability also implies rewards and punishments.[18] One company executive described the punishment theme of accountability with the statement "Individuals who do not perform well simply will not be around too long."[19] Authority and responsibility can be delegated (downwards) to lower levels in the project organization, whereas the accountability usually rests with the individual. Accountability is the summation of authority and responsibility in the sense that when authority and responsibility are delegated, the delegator requires and expects accountability from the delegatee.

Mutual trust between the functional manager and project manager is an important element in successful project management because it can overcome any problem caused due to lack of balance in authority, responsibility, reliability, or accountability. The effect of trust on the growth of a typical project-functional interface bond may progress as follows:[20]

- Initially, due to lack of trust, both project and functional managers may deny that any problem exists, even if there is one.
- As trust develops, both project and functional managers admit shared responsibility; then ...
- Both become willing to meet face-to-face to work out solutions.
- Both project and functional manager begin to formally and informally anticipate problems and prepare themselves to tackle them.
- The communication between both managers becomes sincere and effective.
- They develop a mutual commitment to design strategies that are likely to produce quality results and therefore help each other to win.

Accountability (or visibility as it is sometimes called) is the delegatee's proper response to management's assignment of authority. The accountable staff member provides management with the feedback it needs in order to be reassured that the project is proceeding as it should be. A recognition of accountability, combined with hard work and proper guidance, leads to successful project outcomes. Therefore, the issue of accountability must be considered when designing project organizations.

Putting it all together (authority, responsibility, reliability, and accountability)

Responsibility is the obligation to accomplish whatever is accepted as an assignment. This obligation is twofold: Firstly, the obligation to perform the assigned tasks or duties to the best of one's ability; and secondly, the obligation to account to a higher authority regarding the degree of success achieved in the completion of that assignment.

In general, project managers have the ultimate responsibility and hence are fully accountable for project goals to the client and top management. However, for specific tasks, accountability may flow horizontally or diagonally across the organization. Project managers may choose to retain a part of their responsibility for themselves and/or delegate a part of their work to other project personnel to meet project deadlines. Generally, authority and responsibility flow down the organizational hierarchy or chain of command as they are delegated from one level to the next. Reliability and accountability, on the other hand, move up the organization and normally stop at the person with the formal organizational authority to make changes.

In a project environment, reliability and accountability are interrelated in the sense that reliable people usually meet their accountabilities successfully. Also, when project personnel feel accountable for some project tasks, they feel that they must show self-discipline in reliability and establish a track record in producing high performance. It will not only fulfill their role in accomplishing the assigned work packages but will also give positive feedback to the project manager that the organization is working effectively as a real "team" where everyone is able to work interdependently, produce high quality results, and help each other win.

Appropriate delegation of authority is an important element in organizing and executing projects effectively. After the project objectives are set, activities defined, and the people and other resources organized, project managers must give their key people appropriate authority to meet their responsibilities. In turn, they must require accountability from them in accomplishing project tasks. Project managers would prefer to assign responsibility only to those who are reliable in meeting challenges consistently. Also, when project teams demonstrate reliability in producing quality results, project managers should recognize them for their good performance, providing positive reinforcement and motivating them to further increase their performance.

Responsibility without authority leads to frustration, loss of reliability, and mediocrity. In addition to clear definitions of authority, responsibility, reliability expectations, and accountability, it is important to establish good working relationships between all project participants. The significant time and effort that this requires is well spent at the frond end, while organizing the project.

Delegation in Project Management

The surest way for an executive to kill himself is to refuse to learn how, when, and to whom to delegate work.

— J.C. Penney

As a project evolves, project managers cannot do everything themselves. Consequently, they must delegate their work and responsibility by passing their authority in part, or in total, to another person. Delegating is not easy, yet is one of the most important skills that project managers must learn. It requires effective communication, negotiation and interpersonal skills.

What delegation involves

Delegation is the process by which authority is distributed from the project manager to individuals working on the project. When any of the project team members accept an assignment through delegation from the project manager, they accept new authority and the responsibility for it. The expectation is that the person will be reliable and will be held accountable for performance of the assignment. When project managers delegate authority for any task, they still have the ultimate responsibility for the end results. They also agree to be held accountable for the decision to delegate (i.e., the way the project managers have chosen to handle their responsibility). The act of delegation, therefore, creates a duality of responsibility and accountability that is related to the same task and its execution.

What delegation is not:
- It is not "passing the buck."
- It is not "dumping."
- It is not "puppeteering."
- It is not "dealing with trivia."
- It is not "ego gratification."

Delegation involves:
- Giving responsibility (obligation to perform the assigned tasks)
- Gaining acceptance (the team member's agreement to be responsible)
- Granting authority (the right and power to accomplish the tasks)
- Expecting reliability (assurance of best and consistent effort)
- Requiring accountability (accepting responsibility for success or failure).

In a project environment, the relationships between authority, responsibility, reliability, and accountability in the delegation process can be described as:
- The delegator grants authority and requires accountability from the delegatee.
- The delegator assigns responsibility and expects reliability from the delegatee.

When accountability is met, it leads to accomplishments. When responsibility is fulfilled in a reliable manner, i.e., reliability is demonstrated by quality results, it leads to recognition. The delegation process, used in this way, creates positive reinforcement and enhances motivation in both the delegator and the delegatee to further increase their performance.

To make delegation a "full package," it is important that the delegated work be accepted by the delegatee and that, whenever possible, managers delegate in terms of "objectives or products" rather than "process or procedures."

Delegation process

The process of delegation refers to the effective assignment and acceptance of responsibility and includes establishing clear indication and definition of the tasks or duties to be performed, what results are expected after the tasks are completed, and a clear understanding and agreement regarding how and when progress will be reviewed.

Delegation is the assignment or entrusting of organizational responsibilities and obligations, together with the granting of organizational authority, power, and rights. To begin the process of delegation, project managers must first be clear in their own minds as to the objectives to be accomplished. Then they must break their objectives or tasks into smaller manageable packages and decide what they must and can do themselves and what could be or must be done by someone else.

The concept and process of delegation can be illustrated by the "4D's" model (Drop, Delay, Delegate, and Do),[21] which is based on four questions:

1. *What can be dropped?* Answering this question helps to:
   - choose the activities with low payoffs, and
   - decide on things not to be done on a priority basis.
2. *What can be delayed?* Certain items can be easily delayed without serious consequences. To prioritize:
   - try to be effective rather than efficient, and
   - use a yellow file folder marked OBE (Overcome By Events). The reason for using a yellow folder is that yellow is the color of optimism (you do hope to get to it someday). Sometimes things you drop in this file are overcome by events and are not needed anymore. It is a practical way to approach time management by doing important things first.
3. *What can be delegated?* The answer to this question gets to the real heart of the delegation process. The ability of a project manager to delegate effectively and distribute work to others determines two things:
   - their overall worth to the organization in getting things done through others, and
   - their overall achievements in life, which give them self-satisfaction.
   However, the important question here is, *Does the project manager have someone to delegate to?* These days it is becoming difficult due to downsizing, scarce resources, and tight schedules. In such cases, project managers have to depend upon real teamwork (I help you, you help me).

4. *What must I do?* This is an important point in the delegation process. Here project managers decide what they *can* do and what they *must* do. They should concentrate on things that are most important, urgent, and have high visibility and payoffs. These are the things in the projects that they will be remembered and recognized for. On smaller projects, project managers should address this question at the start and do whatever is necessary to kick off the project and set the stage for success.

Why delegate?

If I could, I would stand on a busy corner, hat in hand, and beg people to throw me all their hours.

— *Bernard Berenson*

Effective delegation is essential in a project environment because of tight schedules and scarce resources. It is important to delegate work in order to increase effectiveness and efficiency in managing a project, reducing the crisis atmosphere. Delegated tasks provide stimulus and opportunities to project team members, improving their participation and interest in the project and possibly opening new horizons for them. In addition, delegation creates more free time for the project manager to work on the most important and critical tasks, as well as, simply, more time to think. Creative thinking by the project manager and interested, challenged project team members helps to avoid the "one-person band" syndrome.

What should or should not be delegated? Although it is useful to delegate, project managers must evaluate what to delegate and what they must do themselves. Project managers should delegate:[21]

- Routines (to get out of comfort zones)
- Tasks that require technical expertise (to offer challenges)
- What someone else can do better (to increase morale)
- Some enjoyable things to others (to motivate)
- Tasks or challenges to vary the routine of those who have boring jobs
- Activities that will allow people to cross-train one another so that they can manage their day-to-day crises (to increase self-confidence)
- Projects involving the critical, visible issues of quality, quantity, cost, and timeliness to self-managed project teams or self-directed teams. These teams will accept the challenge, do a good job, and spread the workload evenly.

What should not be delegated. Project managers should not fully delegate:[21]

- Long range planning (although they should involve others)
- Selection of key team players
- Responsibility for monitoring team's key project or key function
- Task of motivating fellow team members (people value how much the leader cares for them)
- Evaluation of team members (performance appraisals)

- Opportunity to reward team members
- Rituals such as funerals, groundbreaking ceremonies, and celebrations (Successful people suit up and show up!)
- Touchy, personal matters, or crises
- Items that set precedents or create future policies.

In general, project managers should delegate some tasks to free up more time for the things that only they can do. In the past, project managers spent most of their time in planning, organizing, staffing, directing, inspecting, and controlling. But nowadays, to be successful, project managers should delegate these functions to their team members and spend their efforts more on understanding human dynamics, coaching, facilitating, motivating, inspiring high team performance, and managing the external stakeholders.

However, project managers must be careful to set boundaries when delegating tasks to others. They are expected to make tough decisions and therefore should not delegate anything that demonstrates a weakness in decision making. Sometimes project managers should follow the adage, *make a decision and stick to it. Any decision is better than no decision.* They may have to take additional steps to make it right later on. Effective delegators know what their limits or boundaries are when delegating, and what they must handle themselves.

Obstacles to the delegation process

There are three general categories of obstacles that can make delegation in a project difficult.[22]

Obstacles related to the project manager. These obstacles vary from project manager to project manager and are mostly related to management style and level of confidence in the team members. For example, project managers may enjoy using personal authority and therefore resist delegating to project team members, perhaps fearing that others may do a better job. Or they may fear that surrendering some of their authority may be seen by others as a sign of weakness. Other obstacles include:

- Subjects are too confidential to involve others.
- Team members are not sufficiently qualified and capable.
- It takes too long to explain the job to someone else ("it's faster to do it myself").
- "I can do it better."
- "I already delegate enough."
- "I cannot take the risk of getting unsatisfactory results."
- "I will lose track of the progress."

Obstacles related to project team members. Sometimes, even if the project manager wishes to delegate, he or she may encounter some roadblocks from project team members. Team members may be reluctant to accept delegated authority due to fear of failure or lack of self-confidence.

Organizing Projects for Success

The additional responsibility may substantially increase their workload and thus complicate working relationships. Even initially cooperative teams can resist delegation if the project manager does not provide sufficient guidance and support once delegation is made.

Obstacles related to organization. The overall climate of the organization may encourage or discourage the delegation process. For example, in a very small organization, the project manager may have no one to whom to delegate. Or, project team members may be suspicious if top management generally does not encourage delegation and a project manager wants to initiate a change.

How to delegate effectively

In general, project managers carry a heavy burden of responsibility. They cannot do everything themselves and therefore must delegate some of the tasks to others. Successful delegation depends upon interpersonal skills, especially communicating and negotiating skills. This section outlines a practical method and guidelines to delegate effectively in a project environment.

Practical method for effective delegation. There are eight essential ingredients of effective delegation, which can be represented by the acronym (2 x ETFP) which stands for Easy To Follow Procedures. Effective and successful delegation involves four steps, each having two major ingredients.[21]

E	⇒ Entrust	and Enlist
T	⇒ Teach	and Touch
F	⇒ Familiarize	and Follow up
P	⇒ Praise (the Process)	and Participate (in Feedback)

Entrust and Enlist. *Entrust* means to select the right individual for the task and show full confidence in the capacity and ability of that person to perform. *Enlist* means to gain that person's partnership. This can be achieved by explaining the task and its importance and then involving the delegatee in planning. This helps the delegator gain the delegatee's acceptance and hence commitment to perform the task effectively and efficiently. This helps to get the delegatee to "buy into" the project for personal benefit and that of the organization. Delegate in terms of objectives rather than in procedures to encourage creativity. This will challenge, motivate, and instill the delegatee with pride and commitment. Delegators can achieve enlistment by explaining that the task being delegated is critical and important to the project; by demonstrating that they only delegate tasks that they are willing to do themselves; and by approaching with, "I need your help"—expressed genuinely not as lip service.

Teach and Touch. When delegating, project managers may need to teach (or model) certain behaviors to help the delegatees succeed:
- *Time:* Agree on a time line or a deadline (ASAP is too vague!)
- *Tools:* Provide the necessary tools. If necessary, teach the delegatee to use those tools.

- *Trouble:* Help the delegatee identify boundaries and possible sources of trouble. Confirm your availability to help when problems arise.

The concept of "touch" implies empowering people so that they feel a sense of ownership and accomplishment. People need to be "touched" (not literally, but mentally) and excited about the challenges and opportunities of jobs delegated to them. Touching can also be a part of effective communication. While delegating work to someone else, the delegator should touch that person figuratively with his or her eyes. Good solid eye communication signals dedication, compassion, and seriousness.[21]

Familiarize and Follow up. To work together in a true partnership, partners must be familiar with each other's work processes, workloads, and personalities.[21] If project managers show interest in their delegatees' work situations, interests and workload, they will likely return that interest and finish the delegated tasks effectively and efficiently.

The second half of this step emphasizes that old delegation axiom "people respect what you inspect and therefore you should inspect what you expect." Note that sufficient time must be provided to enable the delegatee to accomplish the task. The degree of inspection or follow-up will depend upon the delegatee's maturity and competence.

Praise the Process and Participate in Feedback. Delegating work to others involves some risk because it may not be done the way the delegator would have done it. But it is important to praise the process. Praise the efforts of the delegatee—no matter how successful or unsuccessful the overall outcome of delegation turns out. Thank the delegatee for his or her efforts and give positive reinforcement. Any shortcomings can be pointed out later (after the positive aspects), along with suggestions for correcting them. The delegator should make a list of things that went well, as well as those that did not go so well.

Feedback is a very healthy concept and will help everyone in the project to change, improve, grow, challenge, become more creative and an effective delegator and delegatee. Delegatees should be encouraged to give their input in planning and implementing the delegated task and should be given an opportunity to appraise the delegator.

Effective delegators of tasks ask three simple questions of the people to whom they delegate projects or tasks.[21]
1. What helpful things can I do for the delegatee?
2. How do I avoid interfering with the process of delegation?
3. What else can I do to be an effective delegator?

Practical guidelines for effective delegation. Since delegation generally has several advantages and opportunities, here are some guidelines to delegating effectively in a project environment.
- *Explain* why the tasks are being delegated and what is their relative importance to the project, larger projects, and to organizational goals.

- *Establish* mutually-agreed-upon results and performance standards related to the tasks.
- *Delegate* in terms of objectives rather than procedures. To encourage creativity, give people freedom to pursue tasks in their own way. However, it is important to establish the parameters or limits.
- *Give* team members the authority necessary to accomplish the tasks.
- *Ensure* acceptance from the delegatee. Build team members' confidence in the use of the delegated authority.
- *Provide* continuous support, training, and guidance to the delegatee to assist in the satisfactory completion of delegated tasks.
- *Demonstrate* your confidence and trust in the abilities of project team members by encouraging new ideas and minimizing their fear of failure.
- *Uncover* any obstacles to delegation and develop a plan to minimize the effect of these obstacles.
- *Remember* that people produce the best results when they are having fun and doing what they *want* to do rather than what they *have* to do. Therefore, when possible, delegate tasks on the basis of employee interests.
- *Facilitate* team members' access to information, people, and departments that are not normally available to them. This will demonstrate the project manager's sincerity and confidence in team members and improve task performance.

Project managers must develop certain characteristics to be able to delegate effectively. Among these are a willingness to consider new ideas; to give free rein to project team members, sufficient to carry out their responsibilities and even to learn from their mistakes; trust in the abilities of team members; and a tolerance for failure.[23]

In today's highly competitive market, ability to delegate effectively is the true challenge of the project manager's personal time management. In a project environment where all participants are under constant pressure to meet objectives within scope, time, cost, and quality constraints, they must work as partners with each other. In such an environment, people have to work interdependently, and therefore delegating becomes an essential skill to get things done. Project participants must use the eight ingredients and practical guidelines to delegate effectively.

Effective delegation is vital to a well-functioning project team and an appropriate project organization. The process of delegation involves the effective assignment and acceptance of responsibility and includes a clear indication of the tasks to be performed and the results expected. Communicating these points clearly is crucial to successful delegation.

Summary

One of the key issues of organizing a project is to establish and maintain meaningful authority, responsibility, reliability, and accountability relationships between the project manager, project team members, and other stakeholders in the project. The four elements—authority, responsibility, reliability, and accountability—are very critical in designing project organizations. *Authority* confers the right to impose some degree of obedience. *Responsibility* confers the obligation on the recipient to act with or without detailed guidance or specific authorization. *Reliability* refers to the degree to which the recipient of authority and responsibility can be depended upon, i.e., to respond with sound and consistent effort. *Accountability* in the project context is the extent to which the individual or team of individuals are answerable and must provide visible evidence of their actions. These four elements must be balanced appropriately because these are critical for a smooth flow of work in project organizations.

A project manager is rarely granted all the authority needed to fulfill his or her project management responsibilities. Consequently, the development of *de facto* sources and applications of power based upon knowledge, experience, abilities, interpersonal skills, personality, and ability to build and maintain alliances is required. The project environment is very dynamic. Any complexities, ambiguities, and lack of clarification in authority, responsibility, and accountability can lead to a failure in meeting project objectives.

All personnel associated with the project must be involved in identifying and developing the interfaces, guidelines, and relationships regarding authority, responsibility, reliability, and accountability, thereby gaining their acceptance and commitment to work together as a team. For unique and complex projects, an input from the customer/client may also be both useful and necessary. These guidelines must be documented, reviewed regularly, and modified if necessary throughout the life cycle of the project. A Linear Responsibility Chart (Figure 4.8) is an excellent tool to outline the specifics of authority in project management. It provides a better understanding to project team members of their individual and collective authority, responsibility, and accountability.

Delegation plays a significant role in making an organization work. It is through delegation that project managers may groom themselves and team members for promotions in the organization. Without an adequate, committed process of delegation, there cannot be an effective organization and things easily "fall through the cracks" in the project. Effective delegation leads to positive reinforcement and motivates everyone involved to further increase their performance. Communication skills and interpersonal skills are very helpful in balancing the four issues (authority, responsibility, reliability, and accountability) critical to effective delegation and project organizational design.

Delegation means allowing people to do tasks in their own way, even at the risk of some mistakes. Delegation does not, however, mean abdication of managerial control and responsibilities. It means assigning responsibilities, granting authority, expecting reliability, and requiring accountability. Mistakes should be analyzed and converted into learning experiences for the future. At the same time, a clear message must be communicated that mistakes, beyond a certain degree, are considered "fatal and too serious," and will not be permitted. Delegating while retaining control is the balancing act that every good project manager must learn and practice.

To delegate effectively, project managers can use the 4D's model, which involves answering four questions:

- What can be dropped?
- What can be delayed?
- What can be delegated? and
- What must I do myself?

The common obstacles to delegation, which include obstacles associated with the project manager, project team members, and the organization should be recognized. A practical method for effective delegation, Easy to Follow Procedures (2 x ETFP), should be used. This encompasses eight ingredients grouped in four steps: entrust and enlist; teach and touch; familiarize and follow up; and praise (the process) and participate (in feedback). One can exploit the maximum creativity of the delegatees by delegating in terms of objectives rather than in procedures. In all cases, delegators must show confidence in delegatees and provide full support, resources, and positive reinforcement.

In addition to just showing the hierarchical relationships, the overall design of a project organization should respond to the question: How will the project organization really work? Every effort should be made to achieve a balance between authority, responsibility, reliability, and accountability to gain commitment of all project participants. Project organizational structures should be designed to facilitate open and effective communication among the client, top management, project manager, functional manager, and other project participants.

chapter

5

Outline

Success comes to those who make it happen, not to those who let it happen.

— *Anonymous*

Designing a Project Organizational Structure

MANY ORGANIZATIONS INVOLVED in "management by projects" still don't fully realize the organizational implications of this new form of management.

Every project, regardless of its size, has an organizational structure. And every project is unique in terms of its objectives, problems, constraints, priorities, resources, management styles, and operating environment. Therefore, project organizational structures can take various forms.

There are several factors to consider when designing a project organization. These factors include differentiation, integration, interface management, and the forces influencing the organizational structure. Project managers must analyze and evaluate these factors in terms of their roles, interrelationships, and relative advantages and disadvantages.

There are basically only three types of project structures, which are defined by the level of organizational authority given to the project manager: *functional,* in which personnel are grouped hierarchically by speciality; *matrix,* in which project managers share responsibility with functional managers; and *fully projectized/task force* organizational structure, in which project managers have total authority.

As projects progress through their life cycles, their structures may have to be modified to adapt to changes in activities, priorities, and resources. They should therefore be sufficiently flexible to accommodate their specific needs and constraints. Project managers must design organizational structures to optimize human interaction with minimum barriers; facilitate communications and effective teamwork; provide clear compelling directions; match resources with skills; enhance motivation and trust; and demonstrate effective leadership. ∎

About Organizational Structures

Organizational structures alone do not determine project success; what matters is the commitment to make them work.

Creating a project organization, a vital component of successful project management, can be compared to designing the basic framework of a building. Project structures can take on various forms depending on organizational authority given to the project manager. They may also have to be modified to suit the phase in the life cycle of the project due to changing activities and priorities.

The project organizational structure is also highly influenced by the size, complexity, and diversity of projects. However, it is also important to understand the basic purpose of an organizational structure and the importance of flexibility in designing project organizations.

What is an organizational structure?

Every project organization, regardless of its size or function, has a structure. Organizational structure reduces the uncertainty and confusion that results when people are unaware of the big picture, i.e., how their work fits into the overall activity of the project. Organizational structure refers to designated relationships among resources of the project management system. It represents the pattern of formal authority relationships that exists among groups and individuals by means of a graphical illustration called an organization chart.

Generally, an organization chart shows where each person is placed in the formal structure. Traditionally, an organization chart is drawn in pyramid form, with individuals toward the top of the pyramid having more authority and responsibility than individuals toward the bottom.[1] The relative positioning of individuals within boxes on the organization chart indicates broad working relationships, while lines connecting the boxes designate formal chains of command and lines of communication between the individuals.

What an organization chart does and does not indicate. Figure 5.1 shows a typical organization chart for developing a new product. Like most organization charts, it conveys several characteristics of the organization, for example:[2]

- The vertical authority relationships and reporting relationships that exist between senior staff and subordinates
- The general type of work performed
- The different departments that do the work
- The formal communication channels
- The various levels of management.

Many organization charts imply relative status and prestige of individuals according to their authority in the organization. The various managerial positions in the project organization are represented in chart form

Organizing Projects for Success

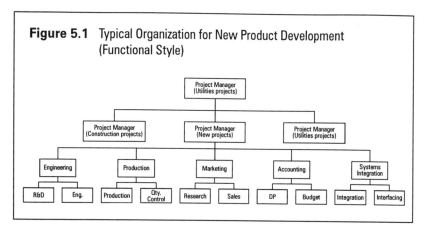

Figure 5.1 Typical Organization for New Product Development (Functional Style)

because the authority structure can be more effectively communicated by a drawing or picture than by words.

However, organization charts do not show all the details of an organization.[3] For example, they do not show in specific terms organizational objectives, significant factors in the organization's external environment, technology used, comparative importance of the jobs in various departments, degree of horizontal interaction occurring between departments, or informal relationships that have arisen spontaneously among workers.[2]

Purpose of a project organizational structure

The general purpose of an organizational structure is to facilitate the use of each organizational resource, both individually and collectively, as the project management system attempts to attain project objectives.[4] An organizational structure should foster human interaction and minimize the conflicts and barriers to such interaction. Project organizational structures can be of various kinds and can be tightened or loosened according to their relative needs. Management styles of top management and the project manager and overall project climate are among the important design factors for managing organizations. Projects must be structured to fit the predominant traits of company culture as well as the personalities and preferences of the key project figures.[5] The larger the project, the greater the likelihood that the structure will be documented and an outline circulated to all major project participants.

A properly designed project organization is essential to project success. Establishing the project structure itself is only a part of organizing the project, while implementing it and making it work is the most critical factor. A project organization structure performs several key functions:[5]

- After being tailored to the specific needs and constraints of the project, it represents a psychological "kick-off," indicating that the project can move ahead at a rapid pace.

- It formally establishes relationships among project manager, project unit managers, project team members, and other project participants.
- It implicitly or explicitly maps out work activities.
- It shows the formal chains of command and lines of communication to guide those who give and receive direction.

Structure and flexibility

As discussed earlier, organization structures depend upon several factors. They must be flexible to suit the style, traits, preferences of project participants and organizational climate. Often, project team members may have opposing positions in relation to project structures:

"What a bureaucracy! I am fed up because I can't get anything to move in this organization."

"You're lucky that there's a bureaucracy to complain about. There doesn't seem to be any organization on our project. I don't know what my responsibility and authority is, where my job stops, and where another person's starts."[5]

The first complaint is a reaction to a rigid structure that conveys information along rigid and formal lines of communication, leading to inefficiency and red tape. This type of structure allows little or no flexibility to expedite the work. The second complaint emanates from a loosely structured project organization characterized by unclear roles and ambiguous responsibilities and authorities. In this type of project organization, flexibility is theoretically infinite or at least so great that work boundaries become blurred and authority and responsibilities are gray areas. This type of project is like the proverbial pot with too many cooks watching over it or, conversely, none at all.[5]

In designing a project structure, the project manager must create one that will meet the diverse project needs at different phases of the project. Too rigid or too loose a project structure may provoke the reactions or typical complaints just described. The project organization's purpose is to facilitate the interaction of people to achieve project goals within specified constraints. According to Lorsch, the design of an organization is composed of the structure, rewards, and project monitoring practices required to direct the behaviors of project team members toward the project goals. The goals of project managers in designing project organizations can be interpreted as follows:[6]

- To create an organizational design that provides a permanent setting in which managers can influence individuals to do their best in completing a particular job
- To achieve the pattern of collaborative effort among individual employees, which is necessary for successful project management

- To create an organization that is cost effective; that is, one that not only achieves the first two goals, but does so with a minimum of duplication of effort, payroll costs, etc.

Just drawing an organization chart does not necessarily mean that the project is organized. In addition to showing (by the chart) who reports to whom (hierarchical relationships), the overall design of the project organization should respond to the question: *How will the project organization really work?*

The organization must facilitate an effective interaction and integration among all the major project participants and achieve open and effective communication among them.

Project Management Factors in Organizing a Project

Project management's challenge is to create an environment that motivates people in their jobs and fosters organizational growth.

Most companies, when deciding to undertake a project effort, define the project in broad terms, appoint the project manager, assign the "necessary" resources and hence claim to be using project management. However, many organizations involved in the "management of projects" still don't realize the full importance of the organizational implications of this new form of management.

Successful project managers create within their project organizations an environment that will facilitate the accomplishment of project objectives. This section outlines the four dominant factors that significantly influence the process of project management, its application, and finally the outcome of project management. Project managers must understand and consider these factors in order to design a project organization that minimizes conflicts and eases the disruptive effects of change in the parent organization as well as in the project.

Differentiation (specialization)

Differentiation refers to the differences or separations that exist across various project units. Lawrence and Lorsch defined differentiation as the state of segmentation of the organization system into subsystems, each of which tend to develop particular attributes in relation to the requirements posed by the relevant external environment.[7] In large projects, the various project units develop their own characteristics because each one is engaged in specialized work. These problems can be resolved by creating specific areas in the project organization where individuals with appropriate skills and experience are grouped together and assigned to find solutions.

In general terms, differentiation is the degree to which departments or project units in a large projects differ in terms of:

- *Structure (flexible to formal).* For example, during the planning phase, flexible and informal structure encourages more creativity, whereas during the implementation phase formal structure may be more helpful.
- *Time horizon (short to long).* R&D activities require a longer lead time and therefore have a longer time horizon versus conventional design or construction-only contracts that have a shorter time horizon.
- *Management style (participative to authoritarian).* Project managers tend to use participative style for creative problem solving whereas they may be inclined to use authoritarian style for well-structured and routine activities.
- *Task environment (certain to uncertain).* For example, R&D and marketing tasks are uncertain whereas manufacturing and distribution tasks have more certainty.

Types of differentiation. Differentiation in a project environment is affected by the types of differentiation (horizontal and vertical) and factors considered in measuring it.

Horizontal differentiation refers to differences among project units or departments at the same level in the project organizational hierarchy: departments or teams primarily involved in design engineering, cost engineering, planning and scheduling, contract administration, and construction.

Vertical differentiation refers to the differences among project units or departments at different levels (top to bottom) in the project organizational hierarchy: differences between project manager, technical team/group leaders, construction supervisor, and construction crew.

Differentiation can be measured by looking at four areas:[8]
- **Differences in goals.** Separate departments will often set separate goals. For example, in an industrial product development project involved in manufacturing and marketing, the production department would prefer standardization to achieve lower unit cost whereas the marketing department would like to have a variety of products to suit many customers, resulting in higher sales.
- **Differences in structure** refer to the extent to which work in departments or project units is rigidly controlled and done "by the book."
- **Differences in time orientation.** Different project departments have different time horizons. For example, production departments are concerned with immediate problems (hourly, daily, or weekly) and production schedules and rates, whereas R&D departments tend to think in longer terms because research activities normally last for months or even years.
- **Differences in interpersonal relations.** The nature of interpersonal relations varies across project units or departments. Under formal project structure, where hierarchy of authority is strictly followed, there is not enough sharing of ideas. Under an open and informal structure,

136

where everyone's input is encouraged, there is more discussion and sharing of ideas.

In combination, the above factors lead to marked differences among project units/departments. In a research laboratory, the goals are more general, the structure is more open, loose, and informal, the time horizon is longer, and there is more emphasis on sharing of ideas and generation of new ideas in order to achieve innovation and creativity. In a construction department, there may be specific goals, a rigid, hierarchical structure, a short time horizon, and little sharing of ideas.

While differentiation allows each project unit or department to maximize their productivity to attain their departmental goals, the dissimilarities may lead to conflict among departments. In general, the greater the differences among departments, the more problems project managers have in getting them to work together (e.g., in a new product development project, marketing with production, R&D with production, etc.).[9]

Integration (coordination)

According to Lawrence and Lorsch, integration is the process of coordination—achieving unity of effort among the various subsystems in the accomplishment of the organization's task.[7] While project managers must divide overall project goals into specific goals for each project unit or department, they must also ensure that the various differentiated departments are coordinated (integrated) so that their efforts contribute to the overall project goals. Integration is the degree of collaboration and mutual understanding required among the various project teams/units to achieve project goals. Most projects are characterized by the division of labor and task interdependencies, creating the need for integration to meet project objectives. This need is greatest between project units that are reciprocally interdependent and least when they are in a pooled interdependent relationship, as discussed under "Technological Factors (Task Interdependence)" in Chapter 3.

According to Koontz and O'Donnell,[10] systems integration is "the essence of management coordination." The purpose of management is the achievement of harmony of individual effort toward the accomplishment of group goals. The project manager's major responsibility is to develop integrating strategies to ensure that a particular system or activity is organized in a way that all of the components, parts, subsystems, and organizational units fit together as a functioning, integrated whole according to the project master plan.

Integration is vital to the success of all projects. Therefore it is important to understand and evaluate strategies for achieving integration, degree of appropriate integration, critical actions of integration, and differentiation versus integration.

Designing a Project Organizational Structure

Strategies for achieving integration. The purpose of integration is to coordinate all project activities, communication systems, and project participants. Strategies for achieving integration can be grouped as vertical coordination strategies and lateral coordination strategies.[8]

Vertical coordination strategies rely on traditional management techniques and vertical information systems to coordinate the activities of the various project units or departments.

- *Traditional management techniques.* Some project managers try to coordinate their project activities by using traditional management techniques such as the chain of command, rules, policies, procedures, objectives, and plans. These techniques may be satisfactory, if the organization does not experience rapid changes in its external environment or technology.

- *Vertical information systems.* A vertical information system sends information up and down the project hierarchy so that better quality decisions can be made. Vertical information systems generally include written reports, teleconferences, computer networks, electronic mail, and so forth.

These strategies allow top management to access large amounts of data needed to make decisions and tend to centralize the decision-making process.

Many organizations make extensive use of a vertical information system. For example, high-tech manufacturing (computers and communication products), telephone companies, and pharmaceutical manufacturers can use sales information to compare the effectiveness of their marketing strategies, advertising, promotions for individual projects or departments, and the organization as a whole.

Lateral coordination strategies are based on the concept that most project organizations must emphasize both vertical and lateral relationships to successfully manage their projects. Lateral relationships are those which develop between the project team members who do not interact through formal lines of authority. Lateral relationships help break down the barriers that may develop between project units or departments due to division of labor. These relationships may either complement or conflict with formal project hierarchical relationships. Because communication is the key in lateral relationships, integration can be considered as mainly a problem of information processing.[11]

Lateral relationships are very effective in spite of the fact that they are not formally recognized on organization charts. Some important lateral relationships happen spontaneously when project team members coordinate their team or unit's work with that of another. But in many cases, project managers must set up systems that are specifically designed to improve lateral coordination. Two of the most commonly used lateral coordination systems are:

138

- *Direct contact* is one of the simplest ways to resolve coordination problems: the relevant individuals simply get together and try to solve a specific problem. This contact often leads to fast, high-quality decisions. For example, an installation crew may face some technical problems in the field while installing some equipment. Such problems can be resolved by getting someone from engineering to meet and help the installation crew, even though the formal organization chart does not recognize this possibility. Trying to resolve this problem by going through formal chains of command would normally take much longer and at much higher cost than using direct contact.
- *Integrators* integrate project activities, which typically run across several functional departments and are done by people with diverse mix of skills and backgrounds. Some activities may fall through cracks and loose ends may not be tied properly if the project manager is not a good integrator.

An integration role is created when contact between two departments or project units is important on a regular basis. An integrator is a person who is normally assigned to coordinate the ongoing activities of various departments or project units whose work is highly interdependent.[12] Integrators (also known as boundary spanners) facilitate coordination between two departments that often interact. A boundary spanner works in one project unit but has a regular contact with another. For example, a person in the system support services departments of a project may be assigned to help users of computing services. This person must have technical knowledge about the computer and systems but should also be able to understand the needs of various users. Other examples of boundary spanners are project coordinators and expediters with very little formal authority.

Sometimes, rather than functioning merely as coordinators, the integrators may have considerable authority over the areas that they are coordinating. In such circumstances integrators, in reality, are mini-project managers. Because of the nature of their work, integrators cannot follow the formal lines of communications in the project organizations if increased efficiency, effectiveness, and less red tape are to be achieved.

- *A task force* is a temporary team of specialists organized to tackle a specific problem or activity involving two or more departments.[12] Each member of the task force represents his or her area and makes logical and unbiased suggestions to solve the problem for the good of the overall project organization. The task force chair directs and focuses everyone's energy towards solving that problem, which should be viewed by everyone as a common objective. The task force is disbanded once the task is completed.
- *Standing committees* are sometimes formed with a mandate to monitor and optimize performance on a long-term basis. Standing committees

may be wrongly perceived as task forces but these are not very effective in a project environment and may frustrate the project participants due to the slow rate of progress.

How much integration? Project managers must be careful not to establish too much or too little integration among various project units. Too little integration will probably lead to the misuse of resources and lower quality decisions because of a lack of an overall direction and focus. Each department may "do its own thing." On the other hand, too much coordination may not be cost effective.[13] With excessive integration, project units or teams may get in the way of each other rather than help each other achieve their goals. Also, if project managers are practicing excessive integration, project team members may feel that the project manager has no confidence in them or they may be wasting too much of their productive time in giving trivial coordinating information to project managers, which reduces overall morale and productivity.

The critical actions of integration. Just as the integration process is a significant component of good project management practice, an integration plan is an important part of the overall project plan. Sometimes an integration plan is a separate comprehensive document, especially if a separate department is responsible for integration. Systems integration is often a separate and important department in the case of large research projects, utilities, computers, and communications projects, and large industrial projects. The project manager is the only person with an overview of the entire system, hopefully from its inception, who can foresee potential interface or integration problems. As a part of the project plan, project managers must develop a clear delineation of the project requirements for reporting, hardware production and delivery, tests and acceptance, and other important milestones. Integration plans should define and identify problems, interface events, and describe interrelationships between tasks and hardware subsystems. The integration plan should then analyze these interrelationships and the scheduled sequence of events in the project.

The integration process consists of a number of critical actions which project managers must initiate and evaluate continually. In most cases, the project manager is the single point of integrative responsibility and is the only person who can initiate these actions. Some of the important actions of integration are:[14]

- *Plan for integration.* Integration doesn't just happen—it must be planned.
- *Develop integrated work breakdown structure, schedule, and budget.* Helps interface management, resource allocation, and reporting.
- *Continually review and update the project plan.* Gives early signals of major problems and variances.
- *Ensure project control and adherence to the project plan.* Avoids unpleasant surprises.

140

- *Ensure design for an integrated system.* Coordinating various design teams right from the outset leads to project success.
- *Resolve conflict situations.* Should be done immediately to avoid problems at organizational and subsystem interfaces.
- *Remove roadblocks.* Project managers should learn to be facilitators.
- *Set priorities.* Defines organizational priority in relation to other projects and project priorities for the utilization of personnel, equipment, and facilities.
- *Make administrative and technical decisions across interfaces.* Helps team members achieve their best.
- *Solve customer or client problems.* Keeps client informed and establishes mutual trust and respect.
- *Assure that project transfer takes place.* Smooth flow from conceptual phase to final delivery and beyond.
- *Maintain communication links across interfaces.* Expedite communication and reduce barriers to communication among project participants.

Differentiation versus integration. Lawrence and Lorsch[7] pointed out that due to rapid advances in technology, increased complexity of projects, and tough global competition, there is an increased need both for greater differentiation (specialization) and for tighter integration (coordination). An effective project manager needs both. However since these two needs are opposed to each other, one is usually achieved only at the cost of the other.[15,16] So it is a question of maintaining the right balance.

Measuring managerial performance. The relationship between differentiation and integration can be described as a tradeoff between these two needs as shown in Figure 5.2. It has been suggested that the ideal high-performance top management or manager falls on the arrow midway between differentiation and integration.[14] Also a line or functional (discipline) manager usually falls closer to the differentiation arrow (because they specialize in certain areas), whereas the project manager falls closer to the integration arrow because he or she has to be more of a generalist and coordinate activities across various functional boundaries. This model illustrates that good project managers must have excellent integrating skills.

The differentiation/integration continuum. As described above, there is a need for both differentiation and integration. Both of these can be measured on a continuum, and the level of differentiation and integration depends upon the organization's task and the environment or climate in which it operates. Figure 5.3 shows an integration/differentiation continuum that combines the uncertainty issues found in most project organizations with the concepts of differentiation and integration.[17]

Every organization can be classified somewhere in this continuum. Every organization must match the demands of its environment. For example, a bureaucratic form of organization is quite appropriate when the relevant technology is well developed, the organizational environment is

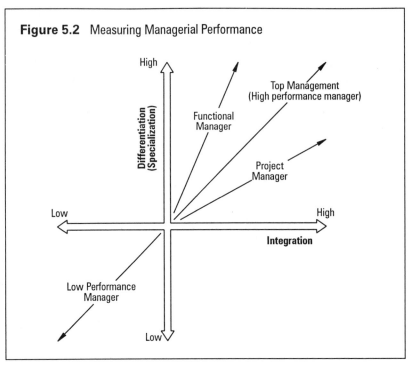

Figure 5.2 Measuring Managerial Performance

Source: Linn C. Stuckenbruck, ed. *The Implementation of Project Management: The Professional's Handbook,* p. 145. © 1981 by Addison-Wesley Publishing Company, Inc. Reading, MA. Reprinted by permission of the publisher.

quite stable, and the rate of change is low (the nature of problems are the same as in the past).

In a bureaucratic structure, both differentiation and integration are low and the organization faces little uncertainty. On the other hand, projects are unique and are specifically developed to cope with rapid and dynamic rates of change, and highly uncertain environments. Adams, Barndt, and Martin indicated these characteristics of a typical project:[17]

- Advanced technology
- Professional personnel
- High levels of uncertainty.

Project-oriented organizations like IBM, R&D organizations, pharmaceutical industries, and high-technology environments have a high level of uncertainty. Therefore, to be successful, high levels of both differentiation and integration are essential.[17]

Interface management

Essentially, interface management implies that the project manager plans, implements and monitors the point of interaction between various elements of the project, the product, and the organization involved.[18] It consists of plan-

142

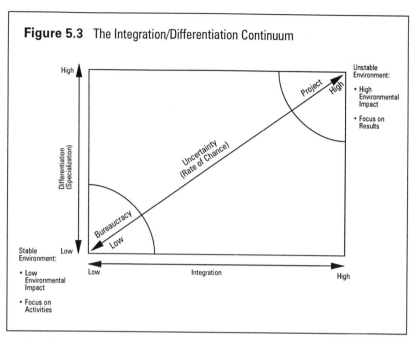

Figure 5.3 The Integration/Differentiation Continuum

Adapted from: John R. Adams, Stephen E. Barndt and Martin D. Martin. 1979. *Managing by Project Management.* Dayton, Ohio: Universal Technology Corp., p. 37. Reprinted by permission of the publisher.

ning, identifying, documenting, scheduling, communicating, implementing, and monitoring interfaces related to both the product and the project.

Typically, project tasks are done by functional managers or people from functional departments and are bound by several interfaces. To manage such projects successfully, project managers must properly manage the interfaces and establish an appropriate communication and working relationship with the functional manager and other project participants. Conflicts between the project manager, functional managers, and other parties involved with the project are also minimized.

Types of interfaces. According to Archibald, there are two basic types of interface in a project environment, which can be further divided into subgroups of which management interfaces are a major division.[18] All project interfaces can be represented as interface events, or points in time that link the project activities. These interface events can normally be identified as management milestones used for monitoring the project progress. The problem of overall project/functional interface is very well discussed by Cleland and King, who point out the complementary nature of project- and functional-oriented organizations.[19] Both are inseparable and closely related, and one cannot survive without the other.

Designing a Project Organizational Structure

Project management, however, is more than just this management interface. It involves three types of interfaces that project managers must manage and continually monitor for potential problems:[14]

• Personal interfaces
• Organizational interfaces
• System interfaces.

Personal interfaces relate to the people working within the project organization. Different people may have different personalities, backgrounds, and norms. Human interfaces, if not managed properly, can lead to personal problems and even conflict. Project managers can obtain the help of functional managers (if people are from the same functional department) or top management (if people are from different disciplines or departments). Project managers may have to act as mediators. In all cases interpersonal skills are very important to resolve personal interface problems which, if not resolved, can be detrimental to project success. These problems become even more difficult when they involve two or more managers.

Organizational interfaces and their management pose a big challenge to project managers, because they not only involve people but also varied goals and conflicting management styles and aspirations. Each organizational unit has its own objectives, disciplines, functions, specialities, and preferred way of doing things. Sometimes organizational units within a project do not understand, appreciate, or share these characteristics with each other, which often leads to misunderstanding, conflict, lack of communication and hence to reduced productivity. Organizational interfaces are more than pure management interfaces since they involve interaction at the working level on a day-to-day basis. Pure management interfaces exist when important management decisions, approvals, or other actions will affect the project. Organizational interfaces also involve additional units outside the immediate company or project organizations, such as the client, contractors, subcontractors, and regulatory agencies on the same or related systems.[14]

System interfaces relate to the product, hardware, facility, construction, or other types of non-people interfaces inherent in the system or subsystems being developed or constructed by the project.[14] The management of system interfaces becomes difficult when the various subsystems are developed by different organizational units. Archibald pointed out two types of these system interfaces.[18]

• *Performance interfaces* exist between subsystems or components of the product. For example, an interface between total output of an automobile engine and other components (such as heating, air conditioning, drive shafts, etc. that consume engine power) represents a performance interface.
• *Physical interfaces* exist between interconnecting parts of the product. For example, interfaces between physical connectors, hoses,

144

and mechanical subassemblies (which join the engine components) and components that use the engine power represent physical interfaces. Another example is an interface between the electrical connectors or plugs (which connect a computer power supply) and power-consuming components.

System interfaces may actually be schedule milestones that transmit the information developed in one task to another task by a specific time. Alternatively, these interfaces may represent the completion of a subsystem on schedule. These can be identified as a responsibility of specific team members and used for tracking the project progress. Interface management is an important skill required in project management. For large projects, involving many disciplines and subsystems, interface management can be described by the more general term *systems integration*, and a special project unit or a group may be specifically assigned to carry out the system integration functions, as discussed earlier under "Critical Actions of Integration."

Forces influencing organizational structure

There are several forces associated with the project task, project manager, project team, and overall environment that influence a project's organizational design. According to Shetty and Carlisle, the formal structure of a project continually evolves throughout its life cycle. Four major forces that influence this evolution are:[20]

Forces in the project manager. These forces refer to the way in which a project manager perceives, identifies, analyzes, and solves organizational problems. Personal background, knowledge, experience, and values influence the project manager's perception of how the project structure should exist or be modified when needed.

Forces in the task. These forces include the degree of technology, uncertainty, and complexity involved in the task. As task activities change (for example, planning activities at the conceptional or front-end phase are different than those during execution phase), a force (in terms of special groups or teams with appropriate expertise) is created to change the project organization as it progresses through its life cycle.

Forces in the environment. These dominant forces include the clients, suppliers and major contractors along with regulatory, political, and social structures affecting the project.

Forces in the project team members. These forces include the personal needs and skill levels of project team members. Obviously, since the project environment and team members vary, forces must be created to change the project organization accordingly.

The design of a particular project organization is actually the result of a complex and dynamic interaction among these forces. Project managers must continually identify, analyze, and balance these forces and be prepared to modify the project organization according to the priorities and phase of the project life cycle.

IN THESE TOUGH ECONOMIC TIMES, management by projects is regarded as a competitive way to manage organizations. However, just appointing a project manager and buying a project management software package are not sufficient to achieve project success. It is important to organize the project appropriately right from the start. To do this, project managers must understand the important project management factors, such as differentiation, integration, interface management,and other forces that can influence the project organization. They must analyze and evaluate these factors to organize the project effectively and meet project objectives.

Forms of Project Organizational Structures

A man carries his success or his failure with him ... it does not depend on outside conditions.

— *Ralph Waldo Trine*

A project organizational structure sets a framework for launching and implementing project activities. Its main purpose is to create an environment in which maximum human interaction can be fostered with a minimum amount of unconstructive conflict. Making a decision as to which form of organizational structure will be used is one of the important aspects of project management. This decision should not be put off, because the whole project operation depends on its organizational form.

Each project is unique. Project organizational structures are aimed at making changes but may sometimes cause disruptions in the existing organization. Therefore, the form of organizational structure should consider the project characteristics *and* the organizational environment in which it will operate. The type of organizational structure chosen may depend on the amount of authority the project manager is given. Project structure can take on various forms with each form having its own advantages and disadvantages. This section deals with the relationship between authority and form of organization; and different forms of organizational structures.

Organizational authority continuum and project structures

Several factors must be considered when deciding on the design of project organizational structures, especially within an existing organization. One method employed in selecting organizational structure is to identify the extent of authority and responsibility top management is prepared to delegate to the project manager.

The basic questions that must be answered by top management in order to design a project organizational structure are:[21]

• How much disruption to the existing organization should be allowed? In other words, how much of a change does top management really want to make?

Figure 5.4 Organization/Authority Continuum

Level of Authority	None	Low	Low to Medium	Medium	Medium High to High	High
Types of Structures	Functional	Weak Matrix (with project expeditor)	Weak Matrix (with project coordinator)	Medium Matrix	Strong Matrix	Fully Projectized/ Task Force
		Matrix (weak to strong)				

- How important is the project or program to the health and future of the company? The answer to this question will influence the amount of power, authority, and responsibility that top management wishes to delegate to the project manager.
- What are the qualifications of the individuals involved?
- How will the project organizational interfaces be handled?
- How will the project be controlled?

There are three basic project structures: functional, matrix, and projectized. Functional structures are not suitable for projects. Normally, projects are organized in a matrix form (weak to strong) or in a fully projectized form. However, there are some additional variations in a matrix organizational structure, depending on the level of formal authority given to the project manager or people involved in managing the projects. Figure 5.4 shows an organization/authority continuum that indicates three main options for project structures corresponding to the level of authority assigned to the project manager.[22]

1. The *functional organization option* refers to a traditional structure in which functional managers have formal authority over most resources. It is only suitable for projects within one functional department. However, it is not suitable for projects that require a diverse mix of people with different expertise from various functional departments. In such cases, the organizational style becomes a matrix.

2. In a *weak matrix with a project expeditor or project coordinator*, management gives some importance to projects and project management process but still gives little authority to the project expeditor or the project coordinator in terms of managing and controlling resources and making decisions. Due to lack of formal authority, project expeditors and project coordinators usually end up doing activities that are more related to project administration than to project management. However, they identify problem areas and facilitate the project management process by using their communication skills, interpersonal skills, and earned power.

Most projects are characterized by multi-disciplinary and cross-functional teams composed of members with different skills and expertise who are assigned to the projects on a full-time or part-time basis. These teams are usually organized in a matrix fashion, with project managers given medium to high decision-making power and formal authority over project resources. The matrix becomes weak to strong as the level of authority increases from low to high (see Figure 5.4).

3. In *fully projectized organizations and task forces*, project managers have a high level of authority to manage and control the project resources and constraints. Task forces and fully projectized organizations are very similar, with the subtle difference that task forces are for short-term projects. Such projects are organized to meet specific mandates or "terms of reference" and deal mainly with studies (social, environmental, etc.) or public inquiries and investigations. On the other hand, fully projectized organizations are relatively more stable and are organized to produce a unique product or service. Like projectized structures, task forces also use expertise from various disciplines and functional areas for specific periods, but the arrangements are more stable in a fully projectized form, which increases the loyalty of participants. Task force members are assigned, full- or part-time, on the basis of their knowledge and skills. They are normally more shielded from organizational politics and external conflicts than personnel in a projectized structure.

The level of authority is therefore an indicator of the type of organizational structure appropriate to meeting project objectives. In a weak matrix structure, the project expeditor has a low level of authority, whereas the project coordinator enjoys a low to medium level of authority to achieve appropriate integration and make decisions. A medium level of formal authority is provided in a medium matrix structure. At the other end of the continuum (see Figure 5.4), in the strong matrix and projectized organizational structures, the project managers typically maintain exceptional control over the project activities and have a specific team assigned to each area.

Common forms of organizational structures

Organizing a project is a complex process. Organizational structure depends on several general and project management factors. Organizational structure must foster effective communication and maximum interactions with minimum conflict and barriers. In addition to several critical factors outlined earlier, style is an important factor for designing organizational structures. The organizational structure can be loosened or tightened; that is, followed in a flexible or rigid manner according to requirements during various phases in the project cycle. For example, during conceptual and detail planning phases, flexibility may encourage more creativity and innovation whereas during the execution and finishing phases, procedures and policies must be followed to optimize the project performance.

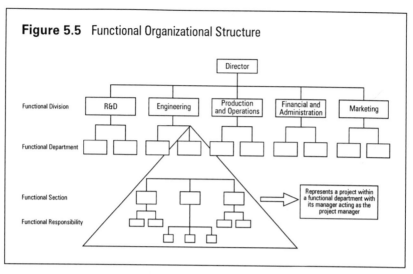

Figure 5.5 Functional Organizational Structure

Adapted from: Harold Kerzner. 1989. *Project Management: A Systems Approach to Planning, Scheduling and Controlling, Third Edition.* New York, NY: Van Nostrand Reinhold, p. 103. Reprinted by permission of the publisher.

The various forms of organizational structures depend upon the relative level of organizational authority given to the persons managing the project. Following are the major forms of organizational structures that can be used for organizing projects of varying size, complexity, and level of uncertainty.

Functional or hierarchical structure. The most prevalent organizational structure found in projects and organizations is a hierarchical, functionally-oriented pyramid with stratified management levels subordinated on distinct horizontal tiers. Project activities are divided functionally by specialities and disciplines. These structures are based on general management theories and classic organizing principles, such as:[22]
- Task specialization
- Line and staff division of responsibility
- Appropriate delegation of authority and responsibility
- Limited span of control.

Specialization (differentiation) is achieved by grouping people based on their functional speciality/discipline (e.g., production, marketing, engineering, accounting). The principle behind the *Doctrine of Specialization* is that it is easier to manage specialists if they are grouped together and supervised by an individual possessing similar skills and experiences.[22]

Figure 5.5 shows a typical functional organizational structure where all individuals in the functional division/department, in theory, report to one person who can initiate a project in that division or department. In a project context, functional structures can be used only for projects belonging to that functional department, for which most of the resources come from that functional department only. There is no project manager in a real sense, but when necessary, the functional manager of that division/department acts as the project manager, using his or her functional authority to direct project activities. As an alternative, the functional manager may assign someone, on a part-time basis, from his or her department itself to act as a project expeditor.

In many cases, the project expeditor is mainly involved in project administration and progress monitoring in a staff capacity. However, if and when the project needs resources from different functional departments, the project organization comes to resemble a matrix style and struggles over the power to control and direct project activities may surface between functional managers and project managers. In spite of such potential problems, functional managers should organize the activities of their department as "projects" and then manage them effectively by using modern project management techniques.

Advantages of functional structure. Functional organizational structures have remained prevalent in business, industrial, and government projects because of several major advantages. They:[2]
- Focus attention on the key functions that must be performed
- Encourage technical competence and specialization of labor by centralizing similar resources
- Provide mutual support by physical proximity
- Provide a career path for people with specialized skills
- Offer clearly defined authority, responsibility, and strong discipline, making it easy for project participants to understand the structure and associated chains of command and lines of communication.
- Eliminate the duplication of activities (because there is only one functional unit for each of the key functions).

Disadvantages of functional structure. Functional organizational structures are not very effective in a multiple project environment because of conflicts that may arise over relative priorities as different projects compete for limited resources. The functional structure may create two potential problems. On one hand, the project is managed by the benefiting functional head, in which case any failure to perform on that person's part is an automatic excuse for others to fail to perform. On the other hand, the project may end up being managed by a committee, with all the dysfunctional characteristics typical of committees.

Consequently, functional structures have the following disadvantages:[2]
- Employees may become overly concerned with their own specialized areas, leading to conflicts among them. For example, marketing and production have different goals; marketing wants to diversify the product line and achieve quick delivery times to maximize sales, whereas

production wants a limited product line and long production runs to minimize production costs.

- No single function is accountable for "overall" project performance.
- Top management may lack the proper training due to over-emphasis on specialization, which leads to employees having a narrow view of the project.
- Coordinating the activities of specialized functions may be difficult because people are preoccupied with their specific functional work. This leads to slow decision making because functional areas still need to get approval from top management for a variety of decision points.
- Coordinating highly specialized functions, all of which hold strong views about their contributions to the project, may be difficult due to professional diversification and personal ego.

To overcome these general deficiencies, management may have to shift from a functional structure to a more integrated one that emphasizes interdepartmental coordination.[23]

Functional organization versus bureaucracy.: The hierarchical or functional organization is an outgrowth of classic bureaucracy. Max Weber, the renowned champion of bureaucracy, claimed that it is technically better than other forms of organization and is indispensable for large, complex enterprises.[24] The functional approach strives to be rational, efficient, and professional by establishing fixed and clear authority relationships and defined spheres of competence.

Although bureaucracy is very close to the hierarchical or functional structure, it has fallen into disfavor. Bureaucracy is associated with negative characteristics such as narrow-mindedness, duplication of effort, irrational rules and policies, and procedures. Functional structures themselves carry with them a certain amount of bad reputation, and score low on the list of favorites for project management.[5]

Functional structures using influence project management. In project management, functional organizational structures are often inadequate to manage multi-disciplinary projects that must be completed within limited schedules and predetermined budgets. Multi-speciality environments call for a horizontal form of coordination, a characteristic that is foreign to vertically oriented bureaucracies or functional/hierarchical structures. However, a lack of lateral flexibility does not make functional organizational structures entirely useless in a project environment. Projects can be managed from a functional base by using the "influence project management" approach.[5]

In this approach, the project is monitored or expedited from a staff position reporting to the general manager, as shown in Figure 5.6. The functional organization remains intact, but the staff member working through the influence of the general manager's position obtains information, follows up, and expedites the project tasks and functions. He or she is often

Designing a Project Organizational Structure

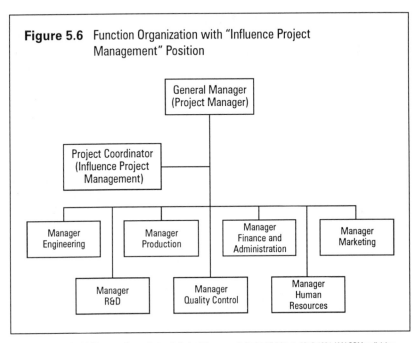

Figure 5.6 Function Organization with "Influence Project Management" Position

able to get good cooperation and resolve problems and conflicts due to this influence and support from a high-level executive.

Sometimes "visibility" can be used as the best tool for supporting weak project management. To have an effective influence on the project management process, the project coordinator sets up a planning room, or hallway, where an easily understood project plan and schedule are displayed. Both the superior and team members can ask questions to make necessary improvements. This is practical because the coordinator starts the ball rolling by producing something that may not be correct but which can now be improved by others.

The person in this staff position must have excellent interpersonal and communication skills. He or she should be careful not to step on sensitive toes and must earn the support of functional managers to create a positive environment and minimize conflicts. If for some reason this approach does not work, the general manager must either take on the role of project manager or revise the project's organizational structure.

Weak-to-strong matrix organizational structures. Most projects require a diverse mix of skills and expertise, which may be fragmented throughout the organization. Due to overall scarcity of resources, matrix structures make use of resources from various functional departments on a full-time or part-time basis to meet project objectives. Although matrix

Organizing Projects for Success

structures are commonly used for managing a project, these have some inherent problems and conflicts. The project personnel work for two bosses: the project manager and the functional manager. This dual authority leads to confusion, divided loyalties, unclear responsibilities, and conflicts over priorities and allocation of resources. In spite of all these problems, a matrix structure is still very practical for applying project management techniques to multi-disciplinary projects. If managed properly, the matrix approach can create synergy through shared responsibility between project and functional managers.

The matrix is weak if the project manager has a lower level of authority than the functional manager to direct and control project activities and resources.[25] A weak matrix can be operated with a project expeditor (with a low level of authority) or with a project coordinator (with a low to medium level of authority). However, due to lack of authority, both the project expeditor and the project coordinator do more project administration than project management. As the project manager's formal authority increases, the matrix becomes stronger (see Figure 5.4). When the organizational authority is high, it becomes very strong, like a fully projectized structure.

Weak matrix (with the project expeditor) refers to a structure wherein persons in charge of projects are given only a little formal authority over the project activities and resources. In such cases, they may be *called* project managers, but they are only able to expedite or administer the project rather than manage it. Moreover, if project managers are technical experts or are more interested in the technical aspects of projects, it will be more efficient and effective for the organization to have a project expeditor who can help in planning and executing project activities.

Figure 5.7 shows an example of an organization with a project expeditor. The project expeditor may act as a staff assistant reporting to a project manager or functional manager who has ultimate responsibility for the project. He or she may work with several project managers and functional managers (manager of engineering or marketing for example) who provide resources for the project. The people working on project activities remain in their respective functional departments and provide services on an "as needed" basis to meet project objectives. The project expeditor does not have much decision-making power but can make recommendations regarding priorities to the general manager and functional managers associated with the project.

The primary responsibilities of the project expeditor in this type of organization are to:[26]
- Identify critical areas with suggestions to resolve problems
- Expedite major components and activities to meet the target schedule
- Forward decisions made by functional and project managers and communicate back any problems, with suggestions to resolve them

Designing a Project Organizational Structure

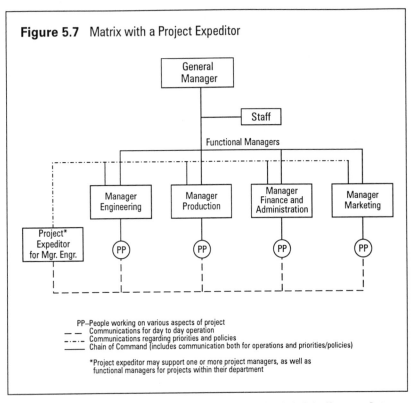

Figure 5.7 Matrix with a Project Expeditor

General Manager

Staff

Functional Managers

Manager Engineering

Manager Production

Manager Finance and Administration

Manager Marketing

Project* Expeditor for Mgr. Engr.

PP

PP

PP

PP

PP–People working on various aspects of project
_ _ Communications for day to day operation
_._._ Communications regarding priorities and policies
_____ Chain of Command (includes communication both for operations and priorities/policies)

*Project expeditor may support one or more project managers, as well as functional managers for projects within their department

Adapted from: John R. Adams, Stephen E. Barndt and Martin D. Martin. 1979. Managing by Project Management, Dayton, Ohio: Universal Technology Corp., p. 43.

- Promote communication among project team members
- Help management monitor the project's progress on a regular basis.

Since, in this type of organizational structure, the project expeditor has no formal authority to make or enforce decisions, he or she must have effective interpersonal skills and technical abilities to help manage project efforts. The project expeditor does not have to motivate project personnel, but must be able to persuade those in positions of authority to keep the project high enough on the priority list that resources will be allocated as needed to meet the project schedule, budget, and quality constraints.

The project expeditor can be used in a matrix organization where project budgets are relatively low and top management wants to try a project management approach.[26] This is particularly effective in high-tech and R&D environments, where persons in charge of projects are scientists or technical experts who may have little interest and experience in implementing the project management process effectively. One project expeditor may support one or more projects, depending upon their size and complexity.

154

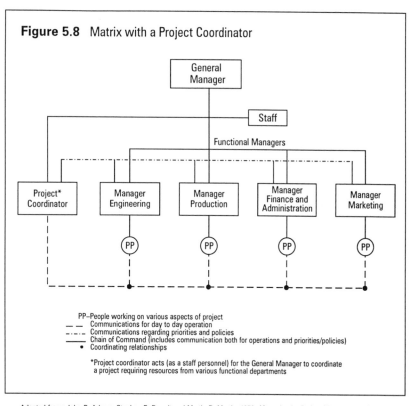

Figure 5.8 Matrix with a Project Coordinator

PP–People working on various aspects of project
_ _ Communications for day to day operation
_._._ Communications regarding priorities and policies
____ Chain of Command (includes communication both for operations and priorities/policies)
• Coordinating relationships

*Project coordinator acts (as a staff personnel) for the General Manager to coordinate
a project requiring resources from various functional departments

Adapted from: John R. Adams, Stephen E. Barndt and Martin D. Martin. 1979. *Managing by Project Management.* Dayton,
Ohio: Universal Technology Corp., p. 44. Reprinted by permission of the publisher.

Weak matrix (with the project coordinator) exists when project managers do more than merely expedite the project. As shown in the organization authority continuum in Figure 5.4, as the parent organization gives more importance to the project, the project expeditor is given an increased level of authority and becomes a project coordinator responsible not just for facilitating or expediting the project, but for coordinating several project activities. Figure 5.8 represents an example of an organization with a project coordinator.[27]

In this case, unlike the project expeditor, the project coordinator reports to a much higher level in the hierarchical echelon, e.g., to the general manager rather than to the functional manager, as shown in Figure 5.8. The characteristics of this form of organization are:[26]

• The project coordinator has authority to assign work to individuals in the functional units after consultation with their direct supervisors and has a significant influence in the decision-making process regarding the priority and allocation of resources to accomplish the project objectives.

- The functional managers may be forced to share authority and resources with the project coordinator, if necessary.
- The functional managers do performance appraisal for project people from their departments but cannot enforce professional or organizational standards regarding project activities.
- Personnel working on the project generally try to satisfy both the project manager and their functional managers.

These characteristics indicate a high likelihood of conflict (especially between the project manager and the functional managers, and between the functional managers and their subordinates now working on the project under the direction of the project manager), which top management must learn to minimize. Kerzner indicated three shortcomings of the project coordinator form of organization, which he referred to as the line-staff form of organization.[28]

1. Upper-level management is not ready to cope with the problems arising from shared authority.
2. Upper-level management is reluctant to relinquish some of its power and authority to the project coordinator.
3. The project coordinator may not have sufficient authority or control to coordinate project activities across several departments involved in the project.

Because of these shortcomings, project coordination is a challenging role and needs sincere support from top management. Also, the project coordinator must have excellent communicating and negotiating skills to minimize conflicts and promote a true team spirit. He or she must be an effective communicator and integrator. In organizations where the project coordinator is selected and used properly, he or she may evolve from "mere existence" to become an important resource. Higher management recognizes and uses the talents of this person to implement appropriate project planning and the project management approach to achieve success.

The concept of using a project expeditor or a project coordinator is quite practical for managing small- to medium-sized projects, especially if a highly competent individual with the right mix of skills can be found to expedite or coordinate the project. It will not only lead to better project management results, but will also increase the productivity of technical experts by allowing them to focus more on technical aspects of the project rather than on project administration, expediting, or coordination.

Medium and strong matrix structures. In reality, neither extreme on the authority continuum—the totally functional or the totally projectized form—is used in managing projects. The compromise lies somewhere in between and, therefore, projects are usually organized in a matrix fashion. Typically, the project manager possesses some, but not total, functional authority for coordinating and integrating project activities. Consequently, a matrix ranges from weak (with a project expeditor or a project coor-

156

dinator) to strong depending upon the level of authority given to the project manager. Medium matrix corresponds to a medium level of authority given to the project manager, whereas in strong matrix the project managers enjoy a high level of authority to direct, coordinate, and integrate project activities and resources. Strong matrix is comparable to a projectized organizational structure.

Fully projectized/task force organizational structure. Because the functional organization has drawbacks, a separate organizational structure for a specific project or program may be established in order to avoid many of the conflicts and problems experienced in the hierarchical or functional organization. As shown in Figure 5.4, projectized and task force organizations are characterized by high levels of authority given to their managers and occupy the other end of the authority continuum.

Projectized and task force structures have more similarities than differences. In both structures, the resources used are the skills and expertise from various functional departments, allocated on a full-time or part-time basis with teams disbanded once the project is complete or the task force meets its mandate. Both the task force chair and the project manager of a projectized organization enjoy a high level of authority to manage and control the resources and constraints. The differences that do exist are very subtle.

- A task force is generally organized to meet specific mandates and terms of reference: conducting environmental or social studies, public inquiries, investigations, and the like. A projectized structure is organized to produce a unique product or service.
- A task force chair is relatively free from functional trappings and enjoy more prestige than managers of projectized organizations.
- The relative degree of complexity in the operating environments of a task force is higher than that of a projectized structure.
- Overall time duration of a task force is shorter whereas projectized structures are more stable in nature, leading to more loyalty from project personnel.
- Task force chairmen are more shielded from organizational politics and external conflicts than managers in projectized organizations.

In terms of level of authority on the organization/authority continuum, both the projectized structure and task force are similar and the differences are minor.

Projectized organizational structure. The project manager in this structure has total authority over the project and can acquire resources needed to accomplish project objectives from within or outside the parent organization, subject only to the scope, quality, and cost constraints identified as project targets.

Figure 5.9 shows a typical projectized organizational structure where personnel are specifically assigned to the project and report directly to the

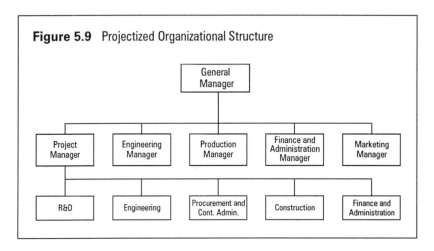

Figure 5.9 Projectized Organizational Structure

project manager (not to their former functional manager). In this structure, the project manager is responsible for the performance appraisal and career progression of all project team members while on the project. This leads to increased project loyalty. As shown in Figure 5.9, the parent organization remains functionally organized, while a temporary and smaller organizational structure is established to meet the objectives of a specific project or program. Personnel from various functional departments are temporarily assigned to the project and provide their services for the duration of the project. The project team consists of those personnel representing the project's functional units.

This type of structure has several advantages:

- Establishes a unity of command and single point of responsibility for the project
- Increases project loyalty
- Promotes more effective informal communication between the project manager and his or her team, and among project team members.

Establishing a new sub-organization with a projectized structure creates some problems as well:

- Duplication of facilities for different projects
- Inefficient use of resources (resources may not be actually needed on a full-time basis throughout the life of the project)
- Project team members "work themselves out of a job."

Project team members have to be assigned to another project or returned to their functional departments. Often those individuals lose their "home" in the functional structure while they are away working for the project. Top management should ensure that this does not affect the career progression of these individuals.[22]

Task force structure. The decision-making capacity of direct contacts is not sufficient when projects involve several departments and their resources. Task forces are formed to handle interdependent tasks on a horizontal basis. A temporary team of specialists, the task force is organized to solve a problem or meet project objectives involving two or more departments. Some of the task force members are full-time while others are part-time. Like projectized structures, task forces exist only as long as necessary and are disbanded once the task force objectives are accomplished or a solution to the problem at hand is developed. Each member of the task force is expected to represent his or her own area and make logical, unbiased suggestions about how to solve the problem.

Task forces are also formed to handle emergencies and some short-term complex projects. A typical task force organizational structure resembles a projectized organizational structure in terms of authority, and also resembles a matrix structure in terms of how it utilizes human resources with varying skills and expertise from various functional departments. However, task forces differ from projectized organizations in terms of complexity, time horizon, functional variety in activities, and freedom from organizational politics. The task force is expected to come up with concrete recommendations that management can act upon.

How to use a task force? Task forces are often used improperly. To ensure that they will be effective, some guidelines should be followed:[29]
- Membership should be representative of those who are knowledgeable about the issues being examined.
- The size of the task force should be limited to six to eight people.
- The mandate of the task force must be clear to the members.
- The role of the leader is crucial. An outside facilitator may be needed to ensure proper discussion of sensitive issues.
- Deadlines must be strictly enforced. The manager who sets up a task force must set realistic deadlines and then let the task force do its work without interference.

Disadvantages of task force structure. While the task force helps focus on the task objectives, it has some significant disadvantages:[5]
- Task forces primarily focus on meeting their mandate or terms of reference, even at the risk of budget overruns, because of their short-term duration and the outcomes being tied to some fixed political or ceremonial schedule.
- Due to its temporary structure, mobilization and demobilization of personnel poses difficulties: Where do the people come from? Where do they go once the task force mandate is completed?
- Difficulty in maintaining a high level of interest and technical expertise occurs because highly specialized experts may turn down temporary assignments.
- Costs of operating in task force environments are high because they are segregated and there may be some duplication of overheads.

Designing a Project Organizational Structure

- Some task force members may not like this form because they feel a social void once the task force is disbanded.

The task force can be a very suitable form of organizational structure for meeting certain mandates or "terms of reference" that involve several departments or types of expertise. It is task-oriented, team-oriented, shielded from organizational politics, unhampered by restrictions imposed by the external organization, and buffered from external conflicts.

Summary

Every project is unique in terms of its size, problems, constraints, diversity of resources, and operating environment. A project structure provides the basic framework for managing a project. Project managers must develop an organizational strategy to fit the needs of a particular project according to its size, complexity, human dynamics, and overall culture of the organization. To manage projects successfully, project managers must design organizational structures that facilitate communication, teamwork, human interactions with minimum barriers, and integration. The project organizational structures must be tailored to fit specific needs and constraints of the particular project.

Project managers must understand and evaluate major project management factors, such as differentiation, integration, and interface management, that have a significant influence on the project organization. Differentiation (specialization) refers to the differences that exist among departments or project units as a result of the different or specialized work they do. These differences require coordination (integration) to meet project goals. Due to rapid advances in technology and increased complexity of projects and systems to be managed, there is an increased need both for greater specialization/differentiation (especially in R&D and high-tech projects) and for integration (tighter coordination) to direct and focus the efforts of the highly specialized personnel to meet the project goals under time, budget, and performance constraints. Vertical and lateral strategies along with some critical actions to achieve effective integration must be used.

Project managers must understand the relationship between differentiation and integration and try to achieve the appropriate balance between these two according to the nature of the project, its people, and the phases of the project life cycle. Project managers must design project organizations to achieve effective interface management in a way that will facilitate the management of personnel, organizational, and system interfaces with minimum problems and conflicts between various organizational units. The forces in the project task, project operating environment, project managers, and the project team members must be identified and analyzed. These forces must be balanced to optimize the overall productivity of all project stakeholders.

Organizing Projects for Success

The successful management of projects is influenced by the organizational structure that optimizes communication, human interactions with minimum barriers, and teamwork. There are three major types of project organizational structures: functional or hierarchical, matrix (ranging from weak to strong matrix), and projectized/task force structures. Each organizational structure has its own advantages and difficulties and is typified by an authority continuum representing the level of formal authority given to the project manager.

For example, functional structures are at one extreme representing no formal authority, and the fully projectized/task force organizations are at the other extreme representing high level of formal authority given to the project manager. The matrix falls between two extremes and the level of authority increases from low to high as the matrix becomes weak to strong. A weak matrix can be operated with a project expeditor or a project coordinator where both of them end up doing mostly project administration rather than project management due to lack of formal authority to direct and control project activities and resources for achieving effective integration. A moderate level of authority is provided in a medium matrix structure. At the other end of the authority continuum, in the strong matrix and fully projectized organizational structures, there exists a project office and the project manager typically maintains exceptional control over the project activities.

In addition to just showing hierarchical relationships, the overall design of the project organization should respond to the question *How will the project organization really work?* Project organizational structures should be designed to facilitate open and effective communication among the client, top management, project manager, functional manager, and other project participants.

It is a funny thing about life; if you refuse to accept anything but the best, you very often get it.

— *Somerset Maugham*

6

Matrix Structure:
Making It Work

A MATRIX ORGANIZATION is one in which there is dual or multiple managerial accountability and responsibility. The matrix organization was developed from a pure projectized form, with the aim of maximizing strengths and minimizing weaknesses. The matrix organization retains the functional (vertical) lines of authority while establishing a relatively permanent horizontal structure designed to interact with all functional units supporting the project. However, the term *matrix* means different things to different people and in different industries.[1,2]

In a matrix, there are usually two chains of command, one along functional lines and the other along project, product, or client lines. Other chains of command, such as geographic location, are also possible.[3] Matrix structures create the problem of two bosses and some other inherent problems which, if not looked after, can cause serious project problems. Most management theorists predicted that the lack of a clearly defined responsibility would lead to managerial ineffectiveness.[4] However, there is no evidence to indicate that multiple authority and role conflict lead to ineffectiveness. For example, the child in a two-parent family has no difficulty with two chains of command—from both mother and father—provided the family is united. ■

Overview of Matrix Organization

None of us can do the job as well as all of us together.

— *Anonymous*

The matrix structure has become a popular model for managing projects in a multi-project environment. However, it is complex and difficult to implement unless the players understand the strengths and weaknesses of this organizational design.

Why the matrix organization?

As we move into the 21st century, project management faces major challenges due to increased global competition and complexities in project organizations. There is an increased need for joint ventures, collaborations, and international projects. The conventional hierarchical (vertical/function) organization cannot cope with the added complexity and the enormous amount of information to be processed. Conventional management theory of "unity of command" offers little help in solving new and unique project problems.

The matrix organizational structure can be used to fill a need for managing multiple and complex projects and programs with limited resources. Figure 6.1 shows a simple matrix organizational structure where resources from several functional departments are assigned to a project on a part-time or full-time basis as needed. The project managers are expected to push the required deliverables horizontally across the functional departments, using resources borrowed from them.

The primary reason for adopting the matrix form in a large organization is that the skills and functions are fragmented throughout the organization. Individual departments cannot solve complex and unique problems because of their narrow viewpoint. This may lead to sub-optimizing or solving the problem within their particular discipline without a "big picture" in mind. According to an old aerospace cliche, "an engineer attacks every problem as if it had an engineering solution." But many projects do not have problems that are purely technical. When the various functional units work in isolation only on their portion of a problem, the work is fragmented and synergy is impossible. It is this fragmentation of resources that the pure projectized organization was developed to avoid. However, it has disadvantages with respect to cost effectiveness, as compared to functional operations.

Most projects require a diverse mix of skills, knowledge, and expertise. The matrix is a practical organizational option because it represents a project structure in which people with different skills and experiences can be brought together to work as a team. In an environment where human resources are scarce, matrix structures make the best use of resources from various functional departments on full- or part-time bases to meet project objectives. These resources may be responsible for doing activities for one

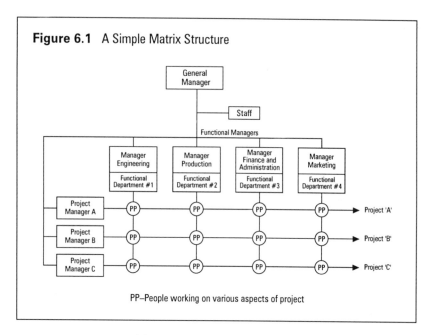

Figure 6.1 A Simple Matrix Structure

PP–People working on various aspects of project

or more projects in addition to their responsibilities in the functional department. Their efforts needed on the project are estimated and negotiated with their functional managers when the project plan is prepared.

Figure 6.2 shows another matrix structure that presents interesting challenges because the workload of personnel is divided among various projects and their functional departments. The matrix structure is an attempt to optimize overall productivity even under this dual and shared responsibility and create a human synergy to meet project objectives, while still maintaining the hierarchical activities of the organization.

Types of matrix

The type of matrix is defined by the level of organizational authority given to the project manager. Either by design or as an outcome of the conflicting forces in the organization, the matrix structure can take various forms.[5,6]

Strong versus weak matrix. The strength or the weakness of the matrix is defined by the authority given to the project manager. The terms "strong" and "weak" should not be interpreted as good or bad organizations. Rather they refer to the relative importance and power of the integrative function in the matrix. The main issue in this context is the balance of power between the functional manager and the project manager.

In some situations, balanced power is not desirable. For example, when a particular project or program is very important to the future of the organization, or the project budget and schedule are very tight, the project

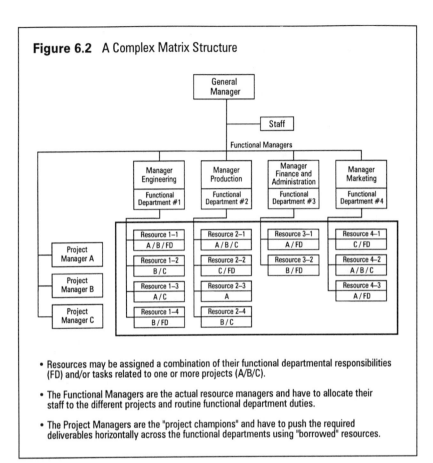

Figure 6.2 A Complex Matrix Structure

- Resources may be assigned a combination of their functional departmental responsibilities (FD) and/or tasks related to one or more projects (A/B/C).

- The Functional Managers are the actual resource managers and have to allocate their staff to the different projects and routine functional department duties.

- The Project Managers are the "project champions" and have to push the required deliverables horizontally across the functional departments using "borrowed" resources.

manager is given a strong positional authority. Sometimes the project manager may feel that with stronger organizational power, he or she will obtain better project performance. For instance, in the construction industry, a strong project office is often necessary to achieve good project control and performance.[7] On the other hand, in some environments, functional management may need more backing. In either case, the balance of power can be shifted in either direction (functional or project management) by changing any one or any combination of three factors.[3]

- The administrative relationship: the levels at which the project and the functional managers report, and the backing that they receive from top management
- The physical relationship: the physical distances between the various people working on the project
- The time spent on the project: the amount of time spent on the project by the respective managers.

166

These three factors determine whether the matrix is strong or weak. A strong matrix is characterized by the balance of power in favor of the project manager, while the balance of power in a weak matrix is definitely in the direction of the functional or line manager. In many project environments, the matrix is modified by shifting the balance of power in favor of the project manager in order to minimize the problems of managing under the "two-boss" system.

The higher up the management hierarchy the project manager reports, plus the more visible the support given by top management, and the more full-time members on the project, the stronger is the matrix structure.

Tight versus loose matrix. Tight versus loose matrix depends on actually splitting the project participants away from their physical reporting relationships with their functional managers. The approach of putting all the project personnel together has been described as a tight matrix, whereas that of widely separated project personnel has been described as a loose matrix.[3] Most project managers would prefer to put all project team members together in the same area, away from their functional bosses. However, this may result in less efficient use of functional facilities and interactions with other functional personnel.

Galbraith has described the managerial alternatives as a continuum ranging from pure functional to pure project structure.[8,9] Matrix falls in the middle of the continuum, ranging from very weak to very strong depending upon the relative balance of power and the amount of decision-making influence possessed by the functional and project managers, respectively.

Project matrix.[5] Although project matrix adopts the matrix organizational format, it is inclined more towards task force philosophy. Project managers or coordinators have more decision-making power than corresponding functional managers. Schedule, cost, quality, and technical performance are strongly emphasized. The project matrix is particularly practical for activities requiring limited technical resources or specialists that can be drawn from an existing pool or respective functional departments. It can be an appropriate structure for certain phases in the life cycle of projects. For example, a team of project personnel may be initiated to come up with the project proposal or front-end planning of some projects. Also, this type of structure can be used for intermediate phases of some projects, when a big project "push" is needed after conceptual designs are done and all technical parameters are finalized.

Functional matrix.[5] Functional matrix is the opposite of the project matrix. In functional matrix organizations, the functional managers have a stronger influence on overall project activities than the project manager or the coordinator. Functional managers tend to emphasize quality at any cost. Consequently, budget and scheduling milestones are ranked lower than the overall quality.

This form of organization normally evolves from a well-entrenched functional organization characterized by tradition and resistance to change, which prevents achieving a better balance. The functional matrix may be appropriate where budget and schedule are less important than overall quality, the majority of the resources come from one functional department, and the number of interactions or interfaces with other departments are minimal. However, on fast-tracking, cost-sensitive projects, the functional matrix tends to lack a goal-oriented attitude.

Balanced matrix.[5] Balanced matrix is the classic matrix typically referred to in project management literature. It distributes authority, influence, and decision-making power between functional managers and project managers or coordinators. This distribution tends to be more horizontal than vertical, with decisions being negotiated among the project participants who are on equal footing with one another. This leads to continuous trade-offs between quality-oriented goals (project, product, or service) and task-oriented goals (budget and schedule). Unfortunately, the degree of conflict tends to be higher in the balanced matrix than in the two other forms (project and functional matrix) because the predominant power is less clearly defined. The balanced matrix is like an ongoing fencing match in which intense competition for decision-making power and influence may continue throughout the project life cycle.

Youker has suggested that the various organizational styles depend upon the level of authority granted to the project manager, with functional organization at one extreme and the pure projectized organization at the other extreme of the authority continuum.[10] Figure 6.3 combines the organizational authority continuum with the organizational continuum,[11] demonstrating that "pure" project, matrix, and functional organizations represent points among an infinite number of organizational options. The organizational continuum is based on the percentage of personnel who are full-time members of the project team and the level of organizational authority assigned to the project manager.[10]

In a pure functional organization, no individuals are specifically assigned to a project team; therefore there is no project manager and no project authority is delegated. However, sometimes in a functional organization the functional manager may initiate a project within his or her own department and act as the project manager as well. If the project requires resources from other functional departments, it comes to resemble a very weak matrix organization where the functional manager may assign someone to expedite the project if necessary. However, the project expeditor has little or no formal authority and most of the authority to set priorities and direct resources and activities rests with the functional manager.

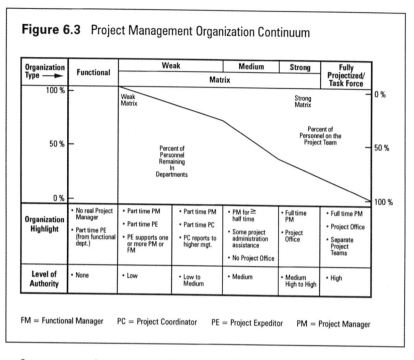

Figure 6.3 Project Management Organization Continuum

Organization Type ➡	Functional	Weak		Medium	Strong	Fully Projectized/ Task Force
		Matrix				
Organization Highlight	• No real Project Manager • Part time PE (from functional dept.)	• Part time PM • Part time PE • PE supports one or more PM or FM	• Part time PM • Part time PC • PC reports to higher mgt.	• PM for ≥ half time • Some project administration assistance • No Project Office	• Full time PM • Project Office	• Full time PM • Project Office • Separate Project Teams
Level of Authority	• None	• Low	• Low to Medium	• Medium	• Medium High to High	• High

FM = Functional Manager   PC = Project Coordinator   PE = Project Expeditor   PM = Project Manager

In a pure project organization, essentially everybody is on the project team and the project manager has essentially total responsibility and authority for the project activities and resources.

On the organizational continuum shown in Figure 6.3 the matrix falls between and includes a variety of organizational alternatives ranging from a weak to a strong matrix. In a weak matrix, there is either a part-time project expeditor (in a staff capacity) to assist in expediting the project or a part-time coordinator who coordinates project efforts across functional departments. As the project authority increases and the part-time coordinator devotes more time to the project, the matrix becomes medium. Eventually, as the project becomes more important, a full-time project manager is assigned and given more authority to carry out the functions of interface management and systems integration for the entire project. A few specialized assistants may be assigned to the project manager and a project office responsible for systems engineering, cost analysis, scheduling, and planning is established, signifying the start of a strong matrix.

In reality, the specific organizational forms discussed above are merely reference points for relating to a large array of intermediate organizational structures found in actual practice.

More About Matrix

Nine-tenths of the serious controversies which arise in life result from misunderstanding.

— *Louis D. Brandeis*

Although matrix is a good approach to using organizational resources effectively because it unites personnel whose skills are otherwise fragmented throughout different functional departments, it does have some inherent problems. Most of these problems stem from the fact that matrix structure violates some of the classic principles of organizational design. To overcome potential problems, it is wise to have some knowledge of the ground rules, and of the advantages and disadvantages of operating within a matrix structure.

When to use matrix?

The matrix organizational design is quite complex and has some drawbacks. Strong justification is required before any project is organized in a matrix fashion and exposed to the interpersonal conflicts and other administrative and organizational problems to which the matrix organization is prone. Solid reasons must offset the risks and the natural human resistance against this complex structure.

Due to the complexity of matrix structures, careful consideration must be given as to where and how the matrix organization fits into the total organization. In general, matrix is considered to be most practical when:[12]

- Complex, short-run products are the organization's primary output
- A complicated design calls for both innovation and timely completion
- Several kinds of sophisticated skills are needed in designing, building, and testing the products, skills that need constant updating and development
- A rapidly changing marketplace calls for significant changes in products, perhaps between the time they are conceived and delivered.

Matrix implementation requires:

- Training in matrix operations
- Training in how to maintain open communications
- Training in problem-solving
- Compatible reward systems
- Role definitions.

There are three basic conditions under which the matrix organization is viable and can be applied effectively.[5]

Pressure for dual focus. Sometimes the client's needs demand the appointment of a central spokesperson or a single point of contact within the organization, even though the work is being accomplished by several functional units. This spokesperson is ideally a project manager or project expeditor, who, by virtue of being appointed, becomes to some extent responsible for the outcome and thus creates the dual focus of project management within a functionally-managed hierarchy.

Pressure for high information processing capacity. The matrix organization can improve the speed and agility of information processing because its horizontal structure and informal patterns of communications facilitate information processing among project participants more than any other form of organizational structure.

Pressure for shared resources: Because of tough competition, tight budgets, and scarce resources, there is increased pressure for sharing project resources among functional units. Even though matrix structure leads to conflicts between project managers and functional managers, it provides a more efficient use of shared resources than a cluster of numerous independent project structures with overlapping redundancies.

The cumulative positive effects of the matrix must be sufficient to offset the negative effects. Top management should be convinced of its advantages and give their full support while relieving functional managers of their fear of losing real power and control. Similarly, project team members should be assured of good career progression opportunities while working on projects.

Ground rules for matrix

The matrix organization attempts to combine the advantages of the pure functional structure and the projectized organization structure. It is ideal for the project-driven organization, such as in construction, pharmaceutical, and software industries.

According to Kerzner,[12] project management is a "coordinative" function, whereas matrix management is a "collaborative" function. In a coordinative organization, work is assigned to specific people or units who specialize in the particular area. In the collaborative or matrix organization, several people work together on the same task(s) and the information is shared. Modern project management emphasizes integration of the efforts of people with different skills who may belong to several functional departments. In the project organization, the project leader has the authority for decision making, whereas in a matrix organization decision making is more distributed.

Following are some of the ground rules for matrix organization:[12]
- Project team members must be assigned to the project tasks that match their skills.
- Conflict resolution must be done quickly and effectively.
- Management must establish effective communication channels and free access to information between managers (functional and project) and among team members.
- Appropriate horizontal as well as vertical channels must exist for gaining commitments.

- Both functional (vertical) and project (horizontal) managers must be prepared to negotiate resources and trade off project objectives with organizational objectives.
- All managers must have input into the planning and control process.
- The horizontal line must be permitted to operate as a separate entity, except for administrative purposes.

These guidelines refer to ideal matrix conditions. Each brings with it advantages and disadvantages.

Advantages and disadvantages of matrix

The matrix approach aims to create synergy through shared responsibility between project and functional managers. Yet this is easier said than done. Since no work environment is the same, no organization will have the same matrix design.

No specific organizational form can be guaranteed to work at all times or to improve productivity in all situations. However, some organizational forms work better than others, particularly if they are designed to meet specific project needs.

Matrix is a practical organizational form for applying project management techniques to multi-disciplinary projects. Most organizations contain some of the ingredients needed for a matrix structure. Some organizations are loosely structured, with informal channels of communication and participative decision making, while others have a rigid structure characterized by formal policies, procedures, and chains of communication. Still other organizations have hybrid structures because most of their projects and programs are multi-disciplinary.

It is vital to sell the matrix concept to top management and all functional managers to ensure their support and commitment to make it work. If everyone involved in a matrix believes in it and is determined to make it work, matrix will help accomplish outstanding project results. The usual reasons for failure of matrix are either foot-dragging or downright sabotage on the part of functional managers or low level supervisors. It only takes one uncooperative functional manager to create problems that must then be resolved at an early stage through active and sincere support from top management.

The advantages and disadvantages of matrix structure are discussed below.

Advantages of matrix structure. Matrix is a complex organizational form that violates certain classic principles of organizing. Yet matrix organization has many advantages that outweigh its principal disadvantage of complexity. Its more universally accepted advantages go beyond the advantages of general project management. The major advantages of matrix structure are briefly described below.[3,5,6,12,13]

172 —

Clear project objectives. The matrix structure not only makes project objectives more visible but also helps balance these with the objectives of the functional organization.

Project integration. The matrix provides a clear and practical mechanism to integrate project subsystems and work packages across functional lines.

Efficient use of resources. The matrix is less expensive than pure project organization because it provides more efficient utilization of company resources. Personnel can be used part-time if desired and hence can be shared between projects. Allocation of resources can be negotiated between the project manager and the functional manager according to the priorities established by the top management.

Effective communication and information flow. Communication and information flow is faster and more effective because of both horizontal and vertical flow. Horizontal flow facilitates project and systems information to pass from one functional unit to another. Vertical flow provides for detailed functional information to pass from project to project and to various levels of management. Useful information is not locked within a single project. People are not always writing memos and letters, as is done in functional organizations. Matrix tends to short-circuit formal communication channels and encourage telephone calls, problem-solving meetings and face-to-face negotiations. Communication channels on the organizational structure are not rigidly followed. Also, since the matrix fosters a consensus approach, everyone participates in decision making, which increases their commitment to implementing the decisions.

Retention of functional specialists. Teams of functional experts and specialists are kept together even though projects come and go. Specialists are able to continually exchange ideas and information; therefore, technology and know-how is not lost when the project is completed. Also, a team of functional specialists, where team members may even be individually working on different projects, leads to synergic effects, resulting in increased innovation and productive output.

High morale. The matrix structure helps increase morale because project team members work together with the intention of helping each other win on a successful project, resulting in visible achievements. They can see the "big picture" more easily, which motivates them to do their best. Also, working with fellow specialists leads to professional development and better training.

Better career progression. Each person retains their functional "home" after project completion, which shows functional specialists a clear career progression up the functional ladder. Also, if project team members find that their talents and interests are multi-disciplinary, they can set their career objectives to become key members of the project office.

Strong problem-solving base. The matrix structure helps develop a strong base with in-depth technical knowledge and experience about a variety of problems. Complex problems can be analyzed and solved. This strong technical and problem-solving base can help all projects as required.

Minimizes job dissatisfaction. Job satisfaction can be enriched by using the matrix. It discourages the bureaucracy that normally exists in functional departments, thereby reducing the frustration experienced by individuals working on the project. Matrix, when structured appropriately for the right situation, reduces the frustrations caused by bureaucracy because of its flexible structure and atmosphere of open communication. It provides professional challenge and an opportunity to work on a variety of projects. This leads to professional development and job satisfaction and hence to higher productivity.

Stress distribution. Because of the horizontal structure and more equality among project team members, stress is better distributed among the project manager, project team members, and the functional managers.

Better response to the client's needs. Matrix structure helps centralize contacts and give coherent responses to clients' questions. The project manager is motivated by the need to obtain information and helps move the project across functional and interdisciplinary boundaries. In a traditional structure, clients are sometimes frustrated by getting unsatisfactory answers from functional managers because there is no single point of responsibility, no one in charge of the whole project and all interfaces.

Development of project managers. Matrix structure provides excellent training opportunities for promising personnel to become project managers because they can be more easily spotted in the multi-disciplinary project environment. A potential candidate with an ability to work across functional boundaries can be transferred to the project office as an assistant project manager and groomed to be a future project manager.

Smoother project shutdown. In a matrix organization, project termination is not as traumatic and painful as it can be in a pure project organization. It is quite normal for there to be large layoffs when a major aerospace or construction project is completed. Since matrix projects are relatively smaller and the people are spread across a whole functional organization, each department has only a few people to redirect.

Reconciles time-consuming technical requirements with the need to get the job done on schedule. The matrix is the epitome of compromise. Rapid changes involving complex technology require technical watchdogs with enough sovereignty to keep the project sound. On the other hand, projects also need aggressive goal-oriented leaders determined to meet project milestones on budget. The sometimes conflicting goals of developing the best technical solution and getting on with the job can cause an unstable equilibrium in the matrix organization. However, if managed properly, matrix under such circumstances can actually optimize a project's resources and requirements.

Elimination of red tape. Excessive protocol, duplicated administrative systems, and extensive rubber-stamping are pushed aside. The matrix gets people moving horizontally across the vertical organizational structure, encouraging project team members to be objective in solving problems. This does not imply that people are always fast and efficient in a matrix. On the contrary, they can sometimes be slow and cumbersome, which stems from the complexity of interacting within a loose network rather than within a rigid bureaucracy.

Disadvantages of the matrix. The matrix organization has some inherent disadvantages and problems. Identifying the problems is half the battle in overcoming them. Davis and Lawrence separated the problem areas of matrix organizational structures into what they called "matrix pathologies."[14] These problems are not unique to matrix structures but seem more prevalent in it. Some of these problems are described below:[3,5,6,12]

Two bosses. This is perhaps the major disadvantage of the matrix and causes the most conflict. Project personnel work for two bosses and can easily get caught in the middle. They may feel a lack of control over their own destiny when continuously reporting to multiple managers. Further problems of conflict can be caused by project personnel playing one boss off of the other.

Complexity. The matrix organization is inherently more complex than either a functional or a pure project organization because it superimposes one structure upon another. This complexity shows itself in the following problems:

- *Difficulties in monitoring and controlling.* It is hard to monitor and control the large number of people or departments involved.
- *Complex information flow.* Both functional and project managers must touch base with each other before making any major decisions in their own areas of responsibility.
- *Fast reaction difficulties.* Project managers may be restricted from achieving fast reaction because of their limited authority and the need to reach consensus. Top management can resolve this by giving more authority to the project manager.
- *Conflicting guidance.* The more complex organization with two lines of authority always leads to conflicting instructions and guidance.

Priorities. A matrix organization with a large number of projects faces real problems with project priorities and allocation of resources. Most functional managers feel that priorities in their own department and resource allocation are their *own* business. Top management must make such decisions. In some cases, this problem is resolved by using a "director or manager of projects" for reassessing project priorities in consultation with top management. This approach is most valuable in resolving conflict and anxiety within the matrix.

Difference in goals. In matrix structures there are problems in balancing the goals of the project (meet objectives under budget and time constraints) and those of the functional units (achieve technical excellence regardless of cost and schedule). This conflict may lead to too much time being spent on design to achieve perfection. Top management must try to maintain the balance between the goals of both the project and the functional units.

Unclear responsibilities. Responsibilities and accountabilities are not clear in matrix organizations because of the emphasis on group/team effort. For people accustomed to clearly-defined chains of command, the matrix looks like a tossup between an organizational mess and a messed-up organization. The matrix creates an atmosphere where everyone shares responsibility for final results, but involvement of so many people can dilute responsibility to the point that no one feels responsible.

Potential for conflict. There is a potential conflict whenever two project managers compete for the same resources. Initially, it may surface as a struggle for power but later may deteriorate into backbiting, foot-dragging, and project sabotage. Conflict and competition may sometimes be constructive and help achieve high performance. However, it cannot be allowed to degenerate into personal antagonism and discord. Conflict on projects is inevitable—the problem in matrix management is keeping it constructive.

Effect of conflict on management. Top management must be concerned about the fact that both project managers and functional managers go through serious conflicts and stress in matrix organizations. Role conflict arising from the "two-boss" situation can produce extensive stress, anxiety, and job dissatisfaction. Project managers must develop a high tolerance for conflict, which is both time-consuming and expensive.

Duplication of effort. In the matrix form, effective communication is vital, but difficult to achieve. Poor communication may result in some duplication of effort, because project organizations may operate independently.

Less cost effective. The matrix organization is not so cost effective on a company-wide basis because more people (especially administrative) are required to manage the projects. Also, more effort and time is needed initially to define policies and procedures, compared to traditional forms.

Middleton identified four additional undesirable results that can develop from the use of the matrix organization and which can affect a company's capabilities.[15]

- Conflicting project priorities and competition for the same expertise may cause instability in the organization and interfere with its long-range interests by upsetting the traditional business of functional organizations.

- Long-range goals may suffer due to overemphasis on meeting objectives of short-term and temporary projects.
- Shifting people from project to project may disrupt the training of employees and specialists, thereby restricting their growth and development within their field of specialization.
- Lessons learned on one project may not be communicated to other projects.

Despite its disadvantages, with proper support from top management and involvement of functional managers, the advantages of matrix structure outweigh the problems. Complexity and conflicts can be turned around to play a positive role, provided everyone is determined to make it work and help each other win. All this makes the matrix a very viable organizational option.

Making the Matrix Work

The meeting of two personalities is like the contact of two chemical substances; if there is any reaction, both are transformed.

— Carl Jung

In spite of the problems and disadvantages of the matrix organization, it is a practical and viable option for complex and multi-disciplinary projects. The successful functioning of the matrix depends entirely on actions and activities of the various people involved within it. This section deals with the basic roles of the major players in a matrix environment along with some useful concepts and ideas that can be implemented to make the matrix work.[3]

Roles of major stakeholders

The four major players, namely, top management, the functional manager, the project manager and the team members must play their roles effectively with a determination to make the matrix work.[3]

Top management must provide real and immediate support to the matrix, including a clear project charter outlining the purpose of any project and the authority and responsibilities of its project manager.

Functional managers must be willing to modify their usual operations and procedures to give projects an appropriate priority.

Project managers must use strong interpersonal and integration skills. The degree of authority given to the project manager depends upon whether the matrix is strong or weak. Project managers must have effective communicating and negotiating skills. Decisions should be made in consultation with functional managers to get their acceptance and hence commitment to achieve the desired project objectives.

Project personnel (team members and other project participants) must adapt to the "two-boss" situation, which can be a traumatic experience for some people when first encountered.

Practical ideas for making matrix work

Resolving the two-boss situation. One of the main disadvantages of the matrix is that people have two bosses (project manager and home or functional manager). This raises a logical question: *Who is the real boss?* Theoretically, it may be possible to divide authority and responsibility almost equally between the project manager and the functional manager and achieve a balance of power between the two. Still, the answer to this question depends on other factors.

For example, the personnel in a matrix structure may consider the line or discipline (functional) manager as their boss because he or she represents a "home base" to which they would normally return after the project is completed. Also performance evaluations and promotions may be determined by functional managers. However, in some cases, project personnel relate so strongly to the overall project that they perceive the project manager to be their real boss. Perhaps there is no real boss, but rather a continually shifting balance of power.[16] To overcome some of these problems, performance evaluations should be done together, by both the project manager and functional manager. In particular, more weight should be attached to the assessment given by the project manager for the time the individual worked on the project.

Balancing power between the functional manager and the project manager. This is at the heart of the operation of the matrix. In practice, it is difficult to divide the responsibilities and authority between the project manager and functional manager. Cleland and King[17] have described the authorities and responsibilities of both project and functional managers to assure a balance of power.

Generally, a responsibility chart can be used to define jurisdictional areas of management.[9,18] Figure 4.8 shows an example of a typical responsibility chart. Such a chart is probably more meaningful than organization charts or job descriptions, especially if it is agreed to after consultation with concerned managers. This process shows any potential conflicts early, allowing them to be resolved before they become too serious.

A responsibility chart indicates where the major responsibilities lie, but it cannot guarantee a balance of power. Projects are done by people, and all people, including managers, are different. Managers have different personalities and management styles. Some managers depend on their persuasive and negotiating abilities while others look for strong support from top management. In addition, power is dynamic and the balance of power changes as the project progresses.[19] Some of the reasons for not being able to achieve a truly equal balance of power between functional and project managers are:

- Project managers get involved in "who will do the task" in order to obtain the best resources for their projects.

- Project managers get involved in technical decisions to ensure that they are sound and are made on schedule.
- Project managers do not evaluate interfaces on a regular basis and consequently they get concerned about how and where the tasks will be done.
- Functional managers take a personal interest in project details and get involved in *what, when, where, who, and for how much money?* because their departments have to perform the tasks according to projected budgets and schedules. They want to ensure that the task is realistically priced and technically feasible.
- If the functional manager's department is slack and/or overloaded, they may unilaterally adjust the amount of work done to fit the departmental (not the project) budget.

Performance appraisal systems. The performance appraisal concept is central to effective management. Performance appraisal is an inherent problem in matrix organizations due to the "two-boss" situation. People working on the project may have loyalties divided between the functional manager and the project manager because, although they work for the project manager during the project duration, they go back to their functional department after the project is complete. The problem is more complicated if there is friction between the project manager and the functional manager or if project managers have no say in performance appraisal of the members working on their projects. This problem can be resolved by modifying the performance appraisal system to allow the project manager to appraise personnel for the duration they worked on the project.

The functional manager must use this input from the project manager to complete the performance appraisal of persons who were assigned to the project manager. The job description of functional managers and project managers must be revised to reflect this concept. Too often, organizations announce that there is going to be a change in responsibilities but no one really changes the job descriptions or performance measurement system to be consistent with the new way of operating in matrix. Such actions will lead to confusion and to lack of trust and cooperation between the project manager and the functional manager. It also reduces the level of motivation, morale, and commitment of project personnel, as they are not sure of how their performance is measured for their efforts on the project. Consequently, it leads to problems and loss of productivity.

Clearly, the responsibilities listed in Figure 6.4 should be used as a basis for discussion.

Under the "management by projects" approach, projects and programs are usually an important part of the activities of a business. The projects and the project manager can significantly influence the financial situation of the company. It may seem that project managers always have the scale of power tipped in their direction, especially in a pure project organization. However, in a matrix organization, this is not the case. Functional

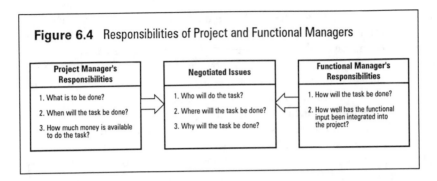

Figure 6.4 Responsibilities of Project and Functional Managers

Project Manager's Responsibilities	Negotiated Issues	Functional Manager's Responsibilities
1. What is to be done?	1. Who will do the task?	1. How will the task be done?
2. When will the task be done?	2. Where willl the task be done?	2. How well has the functional input been integrated into the project?
3. How much money is available to do the task?	3. Why will the task be done?	

managers hold more power since they are perceived to be the real boss by most of the project personnel. Often this is inevitable because functional management represents a ladder in the management hierarchy and is therefore perceived to be more "permanent" by the employees. After all, the functional departments represent a home base to which project personnel may have to return after the project is completed.

Project managers must have strong support from the top management to manage projects successfully in matrix organizations. The project manager must get the job done by available means, even though he or she is not perceived as the real boss. However, appealing to top management too frequently may be counterproductive.

Managing project/functional interface. Although achieving an appropriate balance of power is very important for managing a project matrix organization, it is not sufficient. The type of interface relationship between the project and individual functional manager is the key to a successfully functioning matrix. Every project decision and action must be negotiated across this interface. This interface may create a conflict due to some differences between the objectives of project and functional management. This interface relationship can be one of smooth cooperation or bitter conflict depending upon the personalities, interpersonal skills, and dedication of the respective managers. A domineering personality or power play on the part of one or the other is not the answer. The overpowering manager may win the local skirmish and get things on a short-term basis, but this behavior usually alienates everyone working on the project.

The successful manager is the one who gets things done by working through others. This classic definition is particularly valid for project management in the matrix organization. Cooperation, negotiation, mutual trust, and respect are the keys to successful decision making and management across the project/functional interface. Arbitrary and unilateral decisions can only lead to or intensify conflict. Generally, project managers can accomplish little by themselves; they must depend on the cooperation and support of functional managers.

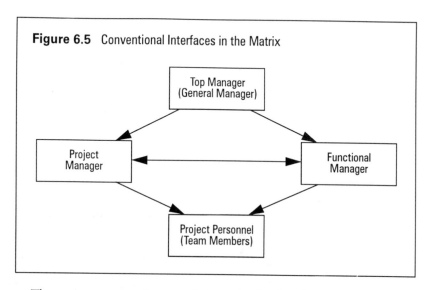

Figure 6.5 Conventional Interfaces in the Matrix

The project manager in a matrix organization has three important interfaces, as shown in Figure 6.5. Project managers need good understanding and support from top management to resolve big problems and remove obstacles. They need good working relationships with functional managers to ensure that most problems are resolved at that level and will not have to go to top management. Project managers must have good understanding, working relationships and cooperation with project personnel and project team members who are working on the project on a temporary basis but may be under direct supervision of their functional managers. The conventional matrix model does not adequately emphasize these important relationships. In a project environment, neither the functional manager nor the project manager can simply give orders and expect results. They must interact with each other and with other players on a frequent basis.

A better organizational model, showing interface relationships as double-ended arrows indicating that these are two-way streets, is illustrated by Figure 6.6. Consultation, communication, cooperation, and constant support are particularly necessary on the part of the project and functional managers. These relationships are keys to the success of any matrix organization and therefore must be carefully nurtured and promoted by top management and by both project and functional management.

There are some salient differences in the roles of the project manager and the traditional functional manager. An analysis of these differences will emphasize the difficulties that occur at the project/functional interface. Cleland and King made such an analysis and indicated that "while these differences are possibly more theoretical than actual, differences do exist, and they affect the manager's *modus operandi* and philosophy."[17]

Figure 6.6 Multiple Management Interfaces

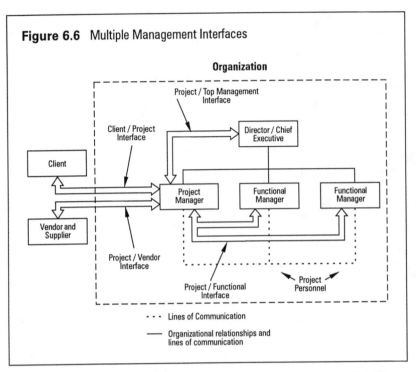

Source: Linn C. Stuckenbruck, ed. *The Implementation of Project Management: The Professional's Handbook*, p. 87. © 1981 by Addison-Wesley Publishing Company, Inc. Reading, MA. Reprinted by permission of the publisher.

The matrix organization is actually a technique for deliberately utilizing conflict positively to get a better job done. Both project and functional managers must work in harmony and help each other win in spite of some conflicting objectives and roles. The project team must be more concerned with solving the problem than with who solves it. Finger-pointing and backbiting only lead to more serious conflicts and lack of productivity. The team concept should not be just lip service but should be nurtured, supported, and implemented. Teamwork and participative problem solving must be emphasized, rather than role definition.

Modification of matrix structure. In small companies having only a few projects functioning in a matrix form, project managers report directly to the general manager. As companies and the number of projects grow, it becomes difficult for the general manager to act as a focal point for all projects. To continue functioning effectively in the matrix form, a new position can be created, that of manager of programs/projects or manager of program/project managers, as shown in Figure 6.7. This frees the general manager from the daily routine of having to monitor all projects personally.

The basic roles of a manager of programs/projects are to:[20]

Organizing Projects for Success

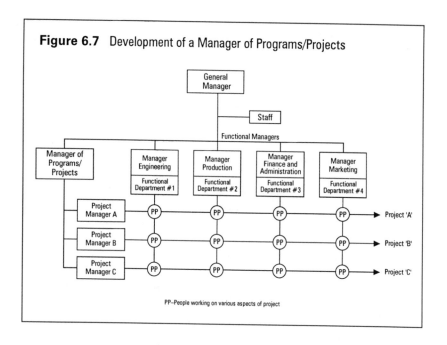

Figure 6.7 Development of a Manager of Programs/Projects

General Manager

Staff

Functional Managers

Manager of Programs/Projects

Manager Engineering — Functional Department #1

Manager Production — Functional Department #2

Manager Finance and Administration — Functional Department #3

Manager Marketing — Functional Department #4

Project Manager A — PP — PP — PP — PP → Project 'A'

Project Manager B — PP — PP — PP — PP → Project 'B'

Project Manager C — PP — PP — PP — PP → Project 'C'

PP–People working on various aspects of project

- Place a greater emphasis on the overview of the project than on its details
- See how projects fit into the overall organizational plan and how project managers interrelate with each other, in other words, keep the big picture in mind
- Resolve conflicts among various project managers in terms of priorities, resources, etc.
- Provide policy, training, consulting, and guidance to the organization on relevant issues
- Provide supervision and training to project management personnel to ensure adequate expertise development, and career advancement opportunity.

In project management, it is hard to say that any one role is more important than another. The manager of programs/projects has overall responsibility for all projects, including directing and leading people and the project management effort; resolving priority conflicts; motivating project teams and other project personnel; and planning for change in the organization. The manager of project managers acts as a liaison between the project management department and top management as well as functional management. He or she acts as an integrator and a systems manager when serving as a liaison. Therefore, he or she must have excellent project management skills, especially human skills.

Using informal matrix.[21] Some projects, especially complex ones such as in R&D environments, are typically arranged in an informal matrix fashion characterized by informal teams and chains of command. Professionals from different functional pools are assigned and spend their working time in one or more interdisciplinary teams led by project managers who are in charge of the respective projects. The informality comes from the *looseness* and *flatness* of a project-oriented matrix which, while necessary to accomplish complex tasks by enhancing technical and scientific communication, cause fewer organizational problems for top management.

The essence of "informal matrix" structure is in its name. The organization can take any form, but the objective is to help the executives manage change. It downplays rigid bureaucratic rules and emphasizes self-regulation. Informal matrix structure discourages petty controls, encourages excellence, and emphasizes decentralized operation with centralized control. [21]

Some common problems of managing projects using informal matrix organization, along with their remedial actions, are described below.[21,22]

Professional egos and divided allegiance. These problems are resolved by giving the appropriate level of importance and freedom to technical specialists. Project managers must be trained in interpersonal skills in order to relate effectively to the professionals who are the life blood of most projects. It is well recognized that it is often good communication and negotiating skill, not hierarchical position, that is persuasive and successful with professionals. A flexible manpower assignment system must be devised that allocates the best talent to projects, while also recognizing professional preferences for challenging assignments. Careful attention should also be given to the selection of key functional managers. They should be respected by professional staff for their technical competence, while also being closely attuned to company goals.

Ambiguous authority and confusing responsibility. These are inherent problems in a typical matrix organization. They lead to a lot of frustration on the part of the project manager, functional management, and project team members.

Informal matrix organizations purposely avoid pyramidal chains of command where directions flow from top to bottom. The wide variety of unique and complex tasks requires the delegation of decision making to project teams that possess the necessary knowledge and a close familiarity with the problems at hand. Maintaining discipline is difficult because professionals in most projects do not see themselves as beholden to a single boss.

While these problems of ambiguous authority will never disappear from the matrix structure, project managers can identify individual responsibilities. This is achieved mainly through discussion and persuasion. Project leaders must clarify *who is supposed to do what, with whom,* and *by when?* Top management must retain responsibility for setting priorities

184

and making the major resource allocation decisions in consultation with functional and project heads during planning meetings.

Technology bias and economic sacrifice. Sometimes, project/matrix organizations are involved in technology transfer and high-technology products in an R&D environment. These projects require a combination of knowledge from several disciplines.

Heavy emphasis on technology and research can seduce professionals into overlooking the economic realities of a project. Discipline-oriented specialists are inclined to see the project in terms of its knowledge challenge, rather than in its budget constraints. Consequently, projects can be over-designed and costs can overrun while compromises are made regarding performance.

Most of these problems can be resolved by focusing on the managerial capabilities of the project manager. The project manager need not be just a strong technical person or a tough budget controller. Rather he or she should have conceptual skills to combine technical savvy with business aptitude in order to maintain professional respect and achieve performance targets. In-house project management training is highly desirable.

Project leaders must apply continuous, realistic planning involving the whole project team to achieve team commitment. Top management must demand informal periodic reviews of major projects, which may involve oral presentations by project managers and their key project members, followed by a thorough probing for hidden problems. Such sessions tend to avoid surprises and make project teams more alert to the need to perform within budget and on schedule.

Interpersonal myopia and team deterioration. The overall effectiveness of a matrix organization depends heavily on smoothly functioning teams. Teamwork is especially critical for tapping the collective intellects of professionals and turning their ideas into successful results. Numerous research studies indicate that technical specialists tend to be "idea" and "thing" oriented, rather than concerned with social relationships.[23] As a result, not all technical specialists collaborate effectively. However, organizational development techniques based on behavioral science, such as sensitivity training and team building,[24] can be applied to improve their interpersonal skills. Project managers must be prepared to encourage constructive behavior. Careful consideration of who is let into the project team is probably the most effective preventive medicine.

Informal matrix organizations should be kept open and flexible (as long as anarchy is prevented). Management should be considered everybody's business, not just the concern of a few at the top. Overall performance can be increased by capitalizing on the intrinsic energies of self-motivated professional and technical staff organized in an informal matrix fashion.

The matrix organizational structure has greatly influenced project management by fulfilling the need for an organization capable of dealing with project size and complexity. Although it increases organizational complexity, it greatly adds to the versatility and effectiveness of project management. The matrix can make project management effective not only for large projects but for small projects as well, and is particularly valuable for solving multi-disciplinary problems.

The matrix organizational form is still popular in the project environment, even though it is not for everyone. A matrix is complex—and it cannot be guaranteed to work. It will only work if the entire organization, from top management to the project personnel, is thoroughly sold on the matrix concept. There are many reasons why the matrix might not work, but failure to lay the groundwork and fully prepare the organization is the principal reason for failure. The major drawback of the matrix is the potential conflict between the functional manager and the project manager. However, its advantages are overwhelming, and its disadvantages are not insurmountable if the matrix is really needed. The matrix will function and result in greatly improved project productivity if top management gives its unwavering support, and functional management and the project personnel accept the matrix as a way of life that can be of great advantage to the company in improving output and profit.

Obviously, the matrix structure is the most complex of all organizational forms. Careful planning and analysis must be done to determine where and how the matrix organization fits into the total organization.

Selecting the Right Organizational Form

The time for action is now. It is never too late to do something.
— *Carl Sandburg*

Projects usually represent a unique set of activities and therefore project management requires special organization. In reality, there is no single unique project organization, but rather a spectrum of organizational alternatives. Even the terms *pure functional, projectized,* and *matrix* do not refer to single clearly defined organizational forms. Each may have many variations depending upon the type and size of the projects involved.

Youker proposed that organizations fit on a continuum of organizational authority, with the functional organization at one extreme and the pure project organization at the other extreme.[10] The matrix fits between these two extremes. As illustrated in Figure 6.3, there are not just these three organizational alternatives, but a whole spectrum of alternatives depending upon the amount of power and authority given to the project manager. Matrix organizations vary from weak to strong. The balance of power tips towards the functional management in the weak matrix and toward the project manager in the strong matrix.

Figure 6.8 Key Factors for Selecting an Organizational Form

Project Characteristic	Matrix			
	Functional	Weak	Strong	Projectized
Uncertainty	Low	Moderate	High	High
Technology	Standard	Standard	Complex	New
Complexity	Low	Low	Medium	High
Duration	Short	Medium	Medium	Long
Size	Small	Small	Medium	Large
Importance	Low	Moderate	Moderate	High
Customer	Diverse	Diverse	3 or 4	One
Interdependency (within)	Low	Medium	Medium	High
Interdependency (between)	High	Medium	Medium	Low
Time Criticality	Low	Moderate	Moderate	High
Resource Criticality	Depends	Depends	Depends	Depends
Differentiation	Low	Low	High	Medium

How is the appropriate organizational form chosen after the decision to implement a project management approach has been made? This section covers some key factors and important questions that must be considered in selecting the right organizational form.

Key factors for selecting the right organizational form

As stated earlier, organizational structures are as unique as the projects, their managers, the parent organization, project participants, and the operating environment. Figure 6.8 presents twelve key factors that should provide assistance in deciding which organizational structure is most appropriate.[7]

By matching the characteristics of the proposed project with the criteria indicated in Figure 6.8, a basic understanding of the most appropriate organizational structures can be achieved. For example, if uncertainty, complexity, time criticality, and importance are relatively high, the technology is complex, the size of the project is large or moderately large, and the duration is expected to be moderate to long, then that project may be an excellent candidate for either a strong matrix or fully projectized organizational structure.

In addition to the decision criteria presented in Figure 6.8, the following factors should also be considered before selecting the final organizational form.

Coordination and commitment. Management must evaluate and explore ways to improve coordination and commitment in the functional structure before moving to a matrix or projectized structure, because it will help avoid disruptions and conflicts normally caused by these structures.

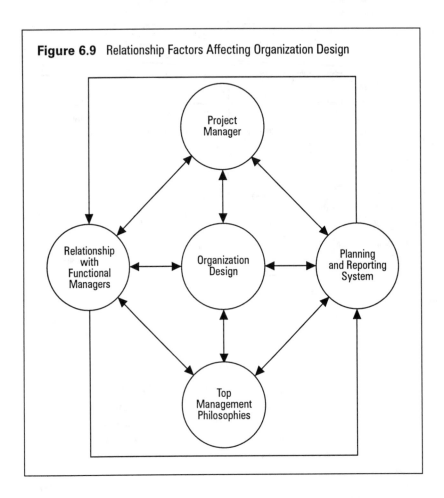

Figure 6.9 Relationship Factors Affecting Organization Design

Matching the matrix type and situation. As described earlier, the matrix structure ranges from weak to strong. Management must determine what variations of the matrix are most suitable for the particular project environment or the situation based on the pros and cons of each variation.

Relationship factors. Finally, management must determine the relationship that exists between organizational design, the abilities of the project manager, and the planning and reporting system of the organization,[10] as shown in Figure 6.9.

For the project organization to be successful, the project manager must possess broad skills, both people and technical, in order to manage the organization towards project completion. The planning and reporting system may be quite simple in a project organization but complex in the traditional functional organization.

188

Important questions for selecting the right organizational form

The organizational form chosen must be appropriate for the company, the project, its management, and the project team. The type of organization needed can also be defined by answering several key questions.[11]

Is the organization ready for project management? The answer depends upon the organization's past successes and/or failures with project management. This helps determine how ready the company is to accept organizational changes and how drastic a change the organization will tolerate without an expensive orientation program.

If an organization is not prepared for a lengthy and expensive orientation and educational program, the project organizational form should be kept as simple as possible. For example, management may start with a project coordinator or a weak matrix, and then try to make that work before advancing further.

How many projects and how big? This refers to the number and size of projects. For example, for a single complex megaproject (in construction, defense, and aerospace industries), a pure project organizational form would be the best choice.

If there are a number of medium-sized projects, a strong matrix is usually a better answer. Whenever there are multiple projects, a matrix should be considered, particularly if the projects are technically complex and cross many disciplinary boundaries. A number of small projects usually suggests the use of multi-project management, in which a single project manager has a number of small projects, none of which justify a full-time project manager. Multi-project management works best when the projects are not complex but are similar or interrelated. A multi-project manager can be valuable in setting priorities and allocating resources.

How complex are the projects? Very complex projects, crossing many disciplinary lines, are usually best managed by a matrix organization. The advantages of the matrix are also apparent when there are a large number of projects, the principal advantage being better utilization of resources—people, equipment, and facilities.

What does the client want? Sometimes the selection of organizational form is influenced by the client or customer, who should be accommodated if at all possible. Government and large construction companies prefer a pure project organization, particularly if it matches their own organization. They like the "mirror image" because all members of the organization know whom to contact as their counterpart in the other organization.

What does top management want? This is the most important consideration. After all, the boss will get her or his way, and therefore the selection of the project management organizational form should be a prerogative and responsibility of top management. In any case, since top management approval is necessary, whoever does the planning should determine what reservations and constraints top management would impose on the project organization. The organizational form selection is often influenced by the style and philosophy of top management and the overall organizational climate.

Unfortunately, top management is not always fully aware of the implications of a proposed project structure. To achieve an effective organizational structure, the project manager should be prepared to give input based upon experience and top management should be prepared to listen with an open mind.

PRACTICALLY, AN ORGANIZATION may use any of the forms of project organization, according to the phases of the project life cycle. The size and importance of the particular project and the authority and responsibility delegated to its project manager, determines the type of organization selected. It is this mix of varying organizational structures that makes the practical application of project management techniques such a complex but challenging undertaking in most large organizations.

> *We all surrender some part of our personality to the organization. The important thing is not so much the organization's pressures as the need to be aware of them. What's devastating is the number of people who find organization ideas superior to their own. They surrender and they enjoy it.*
> — *John Kenneth Galbraith*

Summary

Organizing is a key element of project management. Every project is unique. Project managers must use organizational design strategies that optimize human interactions with minimal barriers to such interactions. Project organizations must aim to facilitate open and effective communication among top management, project managers, functional managers, and other project participants.

The project organizational structure can take different forms, each with its own advantages and difficulties: functional, project expeditor or coordinator, task force, matrix (ranging from weak to strong), and fully projectized organizations, defined by the level of formal authority given to the project manager. Organizational structures may have to be modified to suit the life cycle of the project. A moderate level of authority is provided in a weak matrix structure. At the other end of the authority continuum are the strong matrix and fully projectized organizational structures where the project manager maintains exceptional control over most of the project activities.

The matrix organizational structure combines the advantages of the pure functional and the projectized structure. It emphasizes the collaborative component of project management. It is ideal for multi-disciplinary projects. Matrix structures are designed to use project resources effectively and they tend to improve integration, communication, information flow, the problem-solving base, and response to client needs. Unfortu-

190

nately, due to the "two boss" situation, the matrix structure may become complex and create conflicts between the project manager and the functional manager. Strong interpersonal, negotiation, and communication skills will help in minimizing confusion and conflict and in reaching a win-win situation.

The matrix is becoming the way of life for managing large and complex projects. To make the matrix work, project managers must recognize the roles of various project players, achieve balance of power between the functional and project manager, manage project/functional interface with emphasis on cooperation, negotiation, mutual trust and respect. The team concept should not be just lip service but should be nurtured, supported and implemented. With a large number of big projects, organizations should create a new position of "manager of project management" to coordinate all projects.

For large high-tech and R&D projects, the "informal matrix" approach can be used. This form is characterized by informal teams and chains of command. "Informality" refers to the looseness and flatness of a project-oriented matrix, which can help resolve problems common to the matrix structure and encourage the creative potential of all involved.

It is very important to select the organizational form that is most appropriate for the overall organization, the project, and the project team members. The project organization must be styled to fit the predominant traits of the company culture, as well as the personalities and preferences of key project players. Sometimes a combination of organizational structures may be used, with the structure being modified according to the phase in the project life cycle.

References

Chapter 1

1. Project Management Institute. 1994. *A Guide to the Project Management Body of Knowledge (Exposure Draft)*. Upper Darby, PA: Project Management Institute, pp. 2–3, 38, 60–64.
2. Ralph Currer Davis. 1951. *The Fundamentals of Top Management*. New York: Harper Brothers, p. 268.
3. William H. Newman, et al. 1987. *The Process of Management: Strategy, Action, Results, Sixth Edition*. Englewood Cliffs, NJ: Prentice-Hall, p. 140.
4. Hans J. Thamhain and David L. Wilemon. Leadership Effectiveness in Program Management. In *A Decade of Project Management: Selected Readings from the Project Management Quarterly, 1970–1980*, eds. John R. Adams and Nicki S. Kirchoff, pp. 106–108. Drexel Hill, PA: The Project Management Institute.
5. Paul C. Dinsmore. 1990. *Human Factors in Project Management, Revised Edition*. New York: AMACOM, p. 118.
6. R.M. Wideman. A Framework for Project and Program Management Integration. *PMBOK Handbook, Vol. 1*. Drexel Hill, PA: Project Management Institute, pp. 2–2, 5–5 to 5–7.
7. R.G. Murdick and Fred E. Schuster. Managing Human Resources in Project Management. In *A Decade of Project Management: Selected Readings from the Project Management Quarterly 1970–1980*, eds. John R. Adams and Nicki S. Kirchof. Drexel Hill, PA: Project Management Institute, pp. 101–105.
8. Dinsmore, *Human Factors in Project Management*, pp. 1–2.
9. David L. Wilemon and Bruce N. Baker. 1986. Some Major Research Findings Regarding the Human Elements in Project Management. *Project Management Handbook, Second Edition*, eds. David I. Cleland and William L. King. New York: Van Nostrand Reinhold, pp. 847–864.
10. Dinsmore, *Human Factors in Project Management*, pp. 40–42.
11. Harold Kerzner. 1989. *Project Management: A Systems Approach to Planning, Scheduling and Controlling, Third Edition*. New York: Van Nostrand Reinhold, pp. 10–12.
12. Henry Mintzberg. 1973. A New Look at the Chief Executive's Job. *Organizational Dynamics* (Winter): pp. 20–40.
13. Hans J. Thamhain. 1991. Developing Project Management Skills. *Project Management Journal* (September): pp. 39–44.
14. Michael K. Badawy. 1982. *Developing Managerial Skills in Engineers and Scientists*. New York: Van Nostrand Reinhold.
15. Albert A. Einsiedel, Jr. 1987. Profile of Effective Project Managers. *Project Management Journal* (December): pp. 51–56.
16. Hans J. Thamhain. 1991. Developing Project Management Skills. *The Project Management Journal* (September): pp. 39–44.
17. R.L. Katz. 1974. Skills of an Effective Administrator. *Harvard Business Review* (September–October): pp. 90–102.
18. J.M. Olson and M.P. Zanna. 1991. In *Attitudes and Beliefs in Social Psychology*, eds. R.M. Baron, W.G. Graziano and C. Stangor, p. 196. Fort Worth, Texas: Holt, Rinehart and Winston.
19. See, for example, R.A. Baron and D. Byrne, 1987, *Social Psychology: Understanding Human Interaction, Fifth Edition*, Boston: Allyn and Bacon, p. 116; S.J. Breckler, 1984, Empirical Validation of Affect, Behavior and Cognition as Distinct Components of Attitude, *Journal of Personality and Social Psychology* 47: pp. 1191–1205; and Olson and Zanna, *Attitudes and Beliefs*, pp. 199–212.
20. S. Chaiken and C. Stangor, 1987, Attitudes and Attitude Change, *Annual Review of Psychology* 38: pp. 575–630; J. Cooper and R.T. Croyle, 1984, Attitudes and Attitude Change, *Annual Review of Psychology* 35: pp. 395–426; and A. Tesser and D.R. Shaffer, 1990, Attitudes and Attitude Change, *Annual Review of Psychology* 41: pp. 479–523.
21. Don Hellriegel, John W. Slocum, Jr., and Richard W. Woodman. 1992. *Organizational Behavior, Sixth Edition*. St. Paul, MN: West Publishing Company, pp. 87–96.

22. Paul R. Lawrence and J.W. Lorsch. 1967. *Organization and Environment: Managing Differentiation and Integration*, Boston: Division of Research, Graduate School of Business Administration, Harvard University.

23. Archibald, *Managing High-Technology Programs and Projects*, p. 66.

24. David I. Cleland and William R. King. 1965. *Systems Analysis and Project Management, Second Edition*. New York: McGraw-Hill, p. 237.

25. Linn C. Stuckenbruck. 1981. *The Implementation of Project Management: The Professional's Handbook*. Reading, MA: Addison Wesley, pp. 143–145.

26. David L. Wilemon and John P. Cicero. 1970. The Project Manager: Anomalies and Ambiguities. *Academy of Management Journal* (September).

27. Roger Fisher and William Ury. 1981. *Getting to Yes: Negotiating Agreement Without Giving In*. Boston: Houghton Mifflin.

28. *Webster's New Collegiate Dictionary*. 1977. Springfield, MA: G&C Merriam, p. 228.

29. Richard W. Sievert, Jr. 1986. Communication: An Important Construction Tool. *Project Management Journal* (December): p. 77.

30. David Davis. 1985. New Project: Beware of False Economies. *Harvard Business Review* (March–April): p. 47.

31. Michael C. Thomsett. *The Little Book of Business Etiquette*. New York: AMACOM.

32. Vijay K. Verma and R.M. Wideman. 1994. Project Manager to Project Leader? and the Rocky Road Between. *Proceedings of the 25th Annual Seminar/Symposium*. Upper Darby, PA: The Project Management Institute, pp. 627–633.

33. J.D. Batten, 1989, *Tough-Minded Leadership*, AMACOM; W. Bennis, 1989, *On Becoming a Leader*, Addison Wesley; S.R. Covey, 1991, *Principle-Centered Leadership*, Summit Books; Robert L. Dilenschneider, 1991, *A Briefing for Leaders*, Harper Business; J.W. McLean and W. Weitzel, 1991, *Leadership, Magic, Myth or Method?*, AMACOM; and Kimball Fisher, 1993, *Leading self-Directed Work Teams: A Guide to Developing New Team Leadership*, New York: McGraw-Hill.

34. Batten, *Tough Minded Leadership*, p. 35.

35. McLean and Weitzel, *Leadership, Magic, Myth or Method?*, p. 90.

36. Jeffrey K. Pinto. 1994. *Successful Information System Implementation: The Human Side*. Upper Darby, PA: Project Management Institute, p. 159.

37. M. Dean Martin. 1981. The Negotiation Differential for International Project Management. *Proceedings of the 12th Annual Seminar/Symposium*. Drexel Hill, PA: The Project Management Institute; also published as Chapter 38 in the 1993 *AMA Handbook of Project Management*, Paul C. Dinsmore, ed. New York: AMACOM.

38. Geert Hofstede, 1993, *Cultures and Organizations: Software of the Mind*, New York: McGraw-Hill, pp. 5–14; and also Stephen D. Owen and James Reagan McLaurin, 1993, Cultural Diversity and Projects: What the Project Manager Needs to Know, *Proceedings of the 24th Annual Seminar/Symposium*, Upper Darby, PA: The Project Management Institute, pp. 229–236.

39. Larry Smith and Jerry Haar. 1993. Managing International Projects. In *The AMA Handbook of Project Management*, Paul C. Dinsmore, ed., pp. 441–448. New York: AMACOM.

40. Paul C. Dinsmore and Manuel M. Benitez Codas. 1993. Challenges in Managing International Projects. In *The AMA Handbook of Project Management*, Paul C. Dinsmore, ed., pp. 457–464. New York: AMACOM.

41. Tom Peters. 1992. *Liberation Management: Necessary Disorganization for the Nanosecond Nineties*. New York: Knopf, p. 59.

Chapter 2

1. F.J. Aguilar. 1967. *Scanning the Business Environment*. New York: Macmillan & Co.

2. W.R. Dill. 1958. Environment as an Influence on Managerial Autonomy. *Administrative Science Quarterly* (March): pp. 409–443.

3. H. Mintzberg. 1979. *The Structure of Organizations*. New York: Prentice-Hall.

4. David I. Cleland. 1990. *Project Management:Strategic Design and Implementation*. Blue Ridge Summit, PA: TAB Books., pp. 94–108.

5. David I. Cleland and W.R. King. 1983. *Systems Analysis and Project Management, Third Edition.* New York: McGraw-Hill.

6. W.E. Rothschild. 1976. *Putting It All Together: A Guide to Strategic Thinking.* New York: AMACOM.

7. W.R. King and D.I. Cleland. 1978. *Strategic Planning and Policy.* New York: Van Nostrand Reinhold Co.

8. R.E. Freeman. 1984. *Strategic Management: A Stakeholder Approach.* Boston, MA: Pitman.

9. Aubrey Mendelow. 1985. Stakeholder Analysis for Strategic Planning. In *Strategic Planning and Management Handbook.* New York: Van Nostrand Reinhold.

10. R.M. Wideman, *A Framework for Project and Program Management Integration,* pp. 6.3–6.4.

11. R. Youker. 1992. Managing the International Project Environment. *International Journal of Project Management* (November): pp. 219–226.

12. H. Igor Ansoff. 1965. *Corporate Strategy: An Analytical Approach to Business Policy for Growth and Expansion.* New York: McGraw-Hill, p. 40.

13. W. Wawruck. April 1994. Private communications.

14. J.H. Manley. 1975. Implementation Attitudes: A Model and a Measurement Methodology. In *Implementing Operating Research and Management Science,* eds. R.L. Schultz and D.P. Slevin, pp. 183–202. New York: Elsevier Scientific.

15. D.A. Kolb and A.L. Frohman. 1970. An Organizational Development Approach to Consulting. *Sloan Management Review* 12: pp. 51–65.

16. A Smarter Way to Manufacture: A Special Report on Manufacturing. *Business Week.* April 30, 1990.

17. Kerzner, *Project Management: A Systems Approach,* pp. 696–697.

18. Vijay K. Verma. Creative Leadership: A Key for Managing R&D Programs. *Proceedings of 1989 Northwest Regional Symposium of the Project Management Institute,* pp. 196.

19. L.J. Weber, W. Riethmeier, A.F. Westergard, and K.O. Hartley. 1977. The Project Sponsor's View. *Proceedings of the Ninth Annual Seminar/Symposium of the Project Management Institute.* Drexel Hill, PA: Project Management Institute: p. 70; and also Kerzner, *Project Management: A Systems Approach,* pp. 17–18.

20. Dinsmore, *Human Factors in Project Management,* pp. 45–46.

21. Cleland and King, *Project Management Handbook,* pp. 486–487.

22. H.C. Lucas, Jr. 1979. The Implementation of an Operations Research Model in the Brokerage Industry. In *The Implementation of Management Science,* R.R.L. Schultz and D.P. Slevin, eds. New York: North Holland, pp. 139–154.

23. A.S. Bean and M. Radnor. 1979. The Role of Intermediaries in the Implementation of Management Science. In *The Implementation of Management Science,* R. Doktor, R.L. Schultz, and D.P. Slevin, eds. New York: North Holland, pp. 121–138.

24. R.M. Wideman, *A Framework for Project and Program Management Integration,* pp. 4-5.

25. Kerzner, *Project Management: A Systems Approach,* pp. 14–18.

26. Cleland and King, *Systems Analysis and Project Management,* pp. 351.

27. Harold Steiglitz. 1974. On Concepts of Corporate Structure. *Conference Board Record* 11 (February): pp. 7–13.

28. Louis A. Allen, 1956, Developing Sound Line and Staff Relationships, *Studies in Personnel Policy* 153: pp. 70–80; and also Wendell L. French, 1987, *The Personnel Management Process: Human Resource Administration and Development.* Boston, MA: Houghton Mifflin, pp. 66–68.

29. Cleland, *Project Management:Strategic Design and Implementation,* pp. 242–253.

30. Francis M. Webster. December 1994. Private communication.

31. R.M. Wideman, *A Framework for Project and Program Management Integration.* pp. 6-1.

32. Atigun Project Team. 1993. Atigun Mainline Reroute Project. *PM Network* (January): pp. 9–20.

33. R. M.Wideman. 1985. Good Public Relations: An Essential Part of Successful Project Management, *Proceedings of the 16th Annual Seminar/Symposium.* Drexel Hill, PA: The Project Management Institute, Vol. 1., pp. 6-1.

34. Karen J. Mask and Judith S. Kilgore. 1990. The Westlake Story. *PM Network* (July): 13–18.
35. John R. McMichael. 1994. Boeing Spares Distribution Center: A World Class Facility Achieved through Partnering. *PM Network* (September): pp. 9–19.
36. Henry F. Padgham. 1991. The Milwaukee Water Pollution Abatement Program: Its Stakeholder Management. *PM Network* (April): pp. 6–18.
37. William F. Glueck and Lawrence R. Jauch. 1984. *Business Policy and Strategic Management.* New York: McGraw-Hill, pp. 99–110.
38. Stanley Eitzen. 1974. *Social Structure and Social Problems in America.* Boston, MA: Allyn and Bacon, pp. 12–14.
39. James R. Amdal and Clyde E. Butler. 1994. Partners in Urban Development: The Rebirth of the New Orleans Riverfront. *PM Network* (October): pp. 11–26.
40. Pinto, *Successful Information System Implementation: The Human Side,* pp. 124–125.

Chapter 3

1. Jim Keyser, human resources manager at Coopers and Lybrand Consulting Group, Toronto, quoted in the *Toronto Globe and Mail* (Sept. 14, 1987) p. B-11.
2. Don Hellriegel, John W. Slocum, Jr., and Richard W. Woodman. 1992. *Organizational Behavior, Sixth Edition.* St. Paul, MN: West Publishing, pp. 597–618.
3. Jay W. Lorsch. 1975. *A Note on Organizational Design.* Boston: Harvard Business School, 9-476-094, (Rev. 1977). pp. 1–2.
4. Samuel C. Certo, Steven H. Applebaum and Irene Divine. 1989. *Principles of Modern Management: A Canadian Perspective, Third Edition.* Scarborough, ON: Allyn and Bacon, pp. 193–211.
5. Francis M. Webster, Jr. 1994. PM 101. *PM Network* (December): pp. 44–46. Also Project Management Institute. 1994. *Project Management Body of Knowledge.* Upper Darby, PA: Project Management Institute, p. 63.
6. Frederick A. Starke and Robert W. Sexty. 1992. *Contemporary Management in Canada.* Scarborough, ON: Prentice-Hall Canada, pp. 213–222.
7. Henry Fayol. 1949. *General and Industrial Administration.* Belmont, CA: Pitman.
8. Gerald G. Fisch. 1963. Stretching the Span of Management. *Harvard Business Review* 5, pp. 74–85.
9. See, for example, David Van Fleet and Arthur G. Bedeian, 1977, A History of the Span of Management, *Academy of Management Review*, 3: pp. 356–372; also David Van Fleet, 1984, Empirically Testing Span of Management Hypotheses, *International Journal of Management* 2: pp. 5–10.
10. J. Stieglitz, 1962, Optimizing the Span of Control, *Management Record* 24: pp. 25–29; also M. Keren and D. Levhari, 1979, The Optimum Span of Control in a Pure Hierarchy, *Management Science* 25: pp. 1162–1172.
11. C.R. Walker and R.H. Guest. 1952. *The Man on the Assembly Line.* Cambridge MA: Harvard University Press.
12. J. Mooney. 1953. The Principles of Organization. In *Ideas and Issues in Public Administration,* ed. D. Waldo, p. 86. New York: McGraw-Hill.
13. Eric J. Walton. 1981. The Comparison of Measures of Organization Structure. *Academy of Management Review*: pp. 155–160.
14. E.E. Lawler. 1988. Substitutes for Hierarchy. *Organizational Dynamics*: pp. 5–15.
15. R.H. Hall. 1991. *Organizations: Structures, Processes and Outcomes, Fifth Edition.* Englewood Cliffs, NJ: Prentice-Hall.
16. R.B. Duncan. 1972. Characteristics of Organizational Environments and Perceived Environmental Uncertainty. *Administrative Science Quarterly* 17: p. 314. Also see D.R. Wholey and J. Brittain. 1989. *Characterizing Environmental Variation.* Academy of Management Journal 32: pp. 867–882.
17. F.J. Milliken, 1990, Perceiving and Interpreting Environmental Change: An Examination of College Administrators' Interpretation of Changing Demographics, *Academy of Management Journal* 33: pp. 42–64; and F.J. Milliken, 1987, Three Types of Perceived Uncertainty about

the Environment: State, Effect, and Response Uncertainty, *Academy of Management Review* 12: pp. 133–143.

18. M.A.Hitt, R.E. Hoskisson, and J.S. Harrison. 1991. Strategic Competitiveness in the 1990s: Challenges and Opportunities for U.S. Executives. *Academy of Management Executive* (May): pp. 7–22.

19. I. Wilson. 1985. Evaluating the Environment: Social and Political Factors. In *Handbook of Business Strategy*, W.D. Guth, ed. Boston, MA: Warren, Gorham and Lamont, p. 3-2.

20. H. Mintzberg. 1991. The Effective Organization: Forces and Forms. *Sloan Management Review* (Winter): pp. 54–67.

21. R.E. Hoskisson and T.A. Turk. 1990. Corporate Restructuring: Governance and Control Limits of the Internal Capital Market. *Academy of Management Review* 15: pp. 459–477.

22. L.W. Fry and J.W. Slocum, Jr, 1984, Technology, Structure, and Workgroup Effectiveness: A Test of a Contingency Model, *Academy of Management Journal* 17: pp. 221–246; S.R. Barley, 1990, The Alignment of Technology and Structure Through Roles and Networks, *Administrative Science Quarterly* 35: pp. 61–103.

23. T.H. Davenport and J.E. Short. 1990. The New Industrial Engineering: Information Technology and Business Process Redesign. *Sloan Management Review* (Summer): pp. 11–27.

Chapter 4

1. Cleland, *Project Management: Strategic Design and Implementation*, pp. 160–164, 353.
2. Kerzner, *Project Management: A Systems Approach*, pp. 240–242.
3. Certo, Appelbaum and Divine, *Principles of Modern Management: A Canadian Perspective*, pp. 222–234.
4. J.R.P. French and B. Raven. 1957. The Bases of Social Power. In *Studies in Social Power*, Darwin Cartwright, ed. Ann Arbor, MI: University of Michigan, Institute of Social Research.
5. R. Youker. 1990. Power and Politics in Project Management. Workshop presented at the INTERNET Conference in Vienna, Austria (July); and later published in *PM Network* (May 1991): pp. 36–40.
6. George A. Steiner and William G. Ryan. 1968. *Industrial Project Management*. New York: MacMillan, ©Trustees of Columbia University, p. 24.
7. Cleland and King, *Systems Analysis and Project Management*, pp. 337-338.
8. Certo, Appelbaum and Divine, *Principles of Modern Management: A Canadian Perspective* p. 221.
9. Robert J. Thierauf, Robert C. Klekamp and Daniel W. Geeding. 1977. *Management Principles and Practices: A Contingency and Questionnaire Approach*. New York: Wiley, p. 334.
10. Robert D. Melcher. 1967. Roles and Relationships: Clarifying the Manager's Job. *Personnel* 44 (May/June): pp. 34–41.
11. John H. Zenger. 1976. Responsible Behavior: Stamp of the Effective Manager. *Supervisory Management* (July): pp. 18–24.
12. Certo, Appelbaum and Divine, *Principles of Modern Management: A Canadian Perspective*, p. 225.
13. Cleland, *Project Management: Strategic Design and Implementation*, p. 165.
14. Kerzner, *Project Management: A Systems Approach*, pp. 14–16.
15. Cleland, *Project Management: Strategic Design and Implementation*, pp. 151–156.
16. *New Illustrated Webster's Dictionary of the English Language*. 1992. New York: Pamco Publishing, p. 817.
17. Deborah S. Kezsbom, Donald L. Schilling, and Katherine A. Edward. 1989. *Dynamic Project Management: A Practical Guide for Managers and Engineers*. New York: Wiley and Sons, pp. 184–188.
18. Henry P. Sims, Jr. 1980. Further Thoughts on Punishment in Organizations. *Academy of Management Review* 5 (January), p. 133.
19. How Ylvisaker Makes "Produce or Else" Work. *Business Week* (October 27, 1973): p. 112.
20. Charles L. Buck, Jr. Managing the Most Valuable Resource: People. In *A Decade of Project Management: Selected Readings from the Project Management Quarterly 1970–1980*, eds.

John R. Adams and Nicki S. Kirchof. Drexel Hill, PA: Project Management Institute, pp. 91–95.

21. Mark Towers. 1993. *Dynamic Delegation: A Manager's Guide for Active Empowerment*. Mission, KS: Skill Path Publications, pp. 10, 42–49 and 67–76.

22. Certo, Appelbaum and Divine, *Principles of Modern Management: A Canadian Perspective*, pp. 236–237.

23. Harold Koontz, Cyril O'Donnell, and Heinz Weihrich. 1986. *Essentials of Management, Eighth Edition*. New York: McGraw-Hill, pp. 231–233.

Chapter 5

1. For an interesting discussion of a non-traditional organizational structure, see Pamela M. Banks and David W. Ewing, 1980, It's Not Lonely Upstairs, *Harvard Business Review* (November/December): pp. 111–32.

2. Starke and Sexty, *Contemporary Management in Canada*, pp. 222–225.

3. Harold Stieglitz. 1964. What's Not On An Organization Chart. *Conference Board Record* 1: pp. 7–10.

4. Lyndall Urwich. 1952. *Notes on the Theory of Organization*. New York: AMACOM.

5. Dinsmore, *Human Factors in Project Management*, pp. 97–115.

6. Lorsch, *A Note on Organizational Design*, pp. 1–2.

7. Paul R. Lawrence and Jay W. Lorsch. 1970. *Studies in Organizational Design*. Homewood, IL: Richard D. Irwin, Inc., pp. 89–92.

8. Starke and Sexty, *Contemporary Management in Canada*, pp. 228–232.

9. W.G. Astley and E.J. Zajac. 1990. Beyond Dyadic Exchange: Functional Interdependence and Subunit Power. *Organization Studies*, pp. 11, 481–501.

10. Harold Koontz and Cyril O'Donnell. 1972. *Principles of Management: An Analysis of Managerial Function*. New York: McGraw-Hill, pp. 46–50.

11. J.R. Galbraith, 1974, Organization Design: An Information Processing View, *Interfaces* 4: pp. 28–36; also M.L. Tushman and D.A. Nadler, 1978, Information Processing as an Integrating Concept in Organizational Design, *Academy of Management Review* 3: pp. 613–624.

12. W.J. Altier. 1986. Task Forces: An Effective Management Tool. *Sloan Management Review* 27: pp. 69–76.

13. H.L. Boschken. 1990. Strategy and Structure: Reconceiving the Relationship. *Journal of Management*, pp. 16, 135–150.

14. Stuckenbruck, *The Implementation of Project Management*, pp. 144–155.

15. Paul R. Lawrence and Jay W. Lorsch. 1967. *Organization and Environment: Managing Differentiation and Integration*. Boston, MA: Division of Research, Graduate School of Business Administration, Harvard University.

16. Paul R. Lawrence and Jay W. Lorsch. 1967. New Management Job: The Integrator. *Harvard Business Review* (November-December): pp. 142–151.

17. John R. Adams, Stephen E. Barndt and Martin D. Martin. 1979. *Managing by Project Management*. Dayton, OH: Universal Technology Corp., pp. 33–40.

18. Archibald, *Managing High-Technology Programs and Projects*, pp. 66–68.

19. Cleland and King, *Systems Analysis and Project Management*, p. 237.

20. Y.K. Shetty and Howard M. Carlisle. 1972. A Contingency Model of Organization Design. *California Management Review* 15, pp. 38–45.

21. Stuckenbruck, *The Implementation of Project Management*, pp. 24–33.

22. Robert Youker. 1977. Organizational Alternatives for Project Management. *Project Management Quarterly* 8 (March): pp. 18–22.

23. Marie Day. 1990. Organizational Integration. *Canadian Manager* (Summer): pp. 16–18.

24. Max Weber. 1947. *The Theory of Social and Economic Organizations*, trans. A.M. Henderson and Talcott Parsons. New York: Oxford University Press. Recently, there has been some debate about exactly what Weber was saying about bureaucracy; see R.M. Weiss, 1983, Weber on Bureaucracy: Management Consultant or Political Theorist? *Academy of Management Review* 8: pp. 242–248.

25. Jay R. Galbraith. 1971. Matrix Organizational Designs. *Business Horizons* (February): pp. 29–40.
26. Dwayne P. Cable and John R. Adams. 1982. *Organizing for Project Management*, Drexel Hill, PA: Project Management Institute, pp. 12–18.
27. Adams, Barndt, and Martin, *Managing by Project Management*, pp. 37–45.
28. Kerzner, *Project Management: A Systems Approach*, p. 49.
29. Andrew Campbell. 1987. Task Force Offers Great Potential, But Strong Discipline is Required. *Toronto Globe and Mail* (April 27): p. B7.

Chapter 6
1. Archibald, *Managing High-Technology Programs and Projects*, pp. 14–15.
2. David I. Cleland and William R. King. 1972. *Management: A Systems Approach*, New York: McGraw-Hill, pp. 337–362.
3. Stuckenbruck, *The Implementation of Project Management*, pp. 72–91.
4. J.R. Galbraith. 1977. *Organizational Design*, Reading, MA: Addison-Wesley, pp. 167–171.
5. Dinsmore, *Human Factors in Project Management*, pp. 94–115.
6. Cable and Adams, *Organizing for Project Management*, pp. 18–25.
7. Marc S. Caspe. 1976. An Overview of Project Management and Project Management Services. *Project Management Quarterly* 3 (December): pp. 30–39.
8. J. R. Galbraith. Matrix Organizational Designs. *Business Horizons* (February): pp. 29–40.
9. Galbraith, *Organizational Design*, p. 171.
10. R. Youker, Organizational Alternatives for Project Management. *Project Management Quarterly* 8 (March): pp. 18–24.
11. Stuckenbruck, *The Implementation of Project Management*, pp. 62–64.
12. Kerzner, *Project Management: A Systems Approach*, pp. 115–144.
13. Stewart P. Blake. 1978. *Managing for Responsive Research and Development*. San Francisco: W.H. Freeman and Co., pp. 176–188.
14. Stanley M. Davis and Paul R. Lawrence. 1977. *Matrix*. Reading, MA: Addison-Wesley, pp. 129–144.
15. C.J. Middleton. 1967. How to Set Up a Project Organization. *Harvard Business Review* (March-April): pp. 73–82.
16. John F. Mee. 1969. Ideational Items: Matrix Organization. In *Systems, Organizations, Analysis, Management: A Book of Readings*, David I. Cleland and William R. King. eds, pp. 23–25. New York: McGraw-Hill.
17. Cleland and King, *Systems Analysis and Project Management*, p. 237.
18. R. Melcher. 1967. Roles and Relationships: Clarifying the Manager's Job. *Personnel* (May-June): pp. 34–41.
19. Leonard R. Sayles. 1976. Matrix Management: The Structure with a Future. *Organizational Dynamics* (Autumn): pp. 2–17.
20. Dale R. Beck. 1977. The Role of the Manager of Project Managers. *Proceedings of the Ninth Annual International Seminar/Symposium*. Drexel Hill, PA: Project Management Institute, pp. 139–141.
21. Vijay K. Verma. 1985. *Project Management Techniques and Responsibilities in a Research Environment*. Proceedings of 1985 Northwest Regional Symposium. Drexel Hill, PA: Project Management Institute, pp. C2.5–C2.8.
22. L.E. Greiner, and V.E. Schein. 1981. The Paradox of Managing a Project Oriented Matrix: Establishing Coherence Within Chaos. *Sloan Management Review* (Winter): pp. 17–22.
23. H. Peter. 1957. *Human Factors in Research Administration in Some Applications of Behavioral Research*, eds. R. Likert and S.P. Hager, Jr. New York: UNESCO.

Index

The Human Aspects of Project Management Series

Book 1: Organizing Projects for Success

There is no exercise better for the heart than reaching out and lifting people up.
— *Anonymous*

This book presents an overview of project human resource management, a model for effective management of project human resources, tips for managing external and internal project stakeholders, and organizational design strategies.

Readers will learn to develop an appropriate project organizational strategy, one that effectively interfaces project stakeholders and organizes human resources in a way that inspires high performance among all participants.

Book 2: Human Resource Skills for Project Managers

I will pay more for the ability to deal with people than any other ability under the sun.
— *John D. Rockefeller*

People are the backbone of projects and the most important resources in a project. To survive and grow in the 21st century, project managers must learn and use appropriate human skills to motivate and inspire all those involved in the project. This book focuses on major human skills: communication; motivation; negotiation; conflict resolution; managing conflict and stress; leadership; and power, influence and politics in a project environment.

Readers are presented an overview of major human relations topics along with practical guidelines that can be used to develop and implement the human skills appropriate to project management.

Book 3: Managing the Project Team

Working together, ordinary people can perform extraordinary feats. They can lift things that come into their hands a little higher, a little further on toward the heights of excellence.

Today project managers operate in a global environment and work on joint projects characterized by cultural diversity. Teamwork is the key to project success. This book focuses on developing and sustaining the project team throughout the project life cycle and promotes working together interdependently in a climate of mutual trust and a win/win atmosphere.

This book will help readers to understand the stages of team development; build strong project teams by eliminating barriers to high performance; select and organize the project team for success by gaining commitment through participative decision making; and develop a matching skill and responsibility matrix. After reading this book, project leaders should be able to create an environment to facilitate open and effective communication; develop trust and motivation within the project team and develop appropriate team leadership styles and strategies to suit the project.